Calligraphy Writing Paper

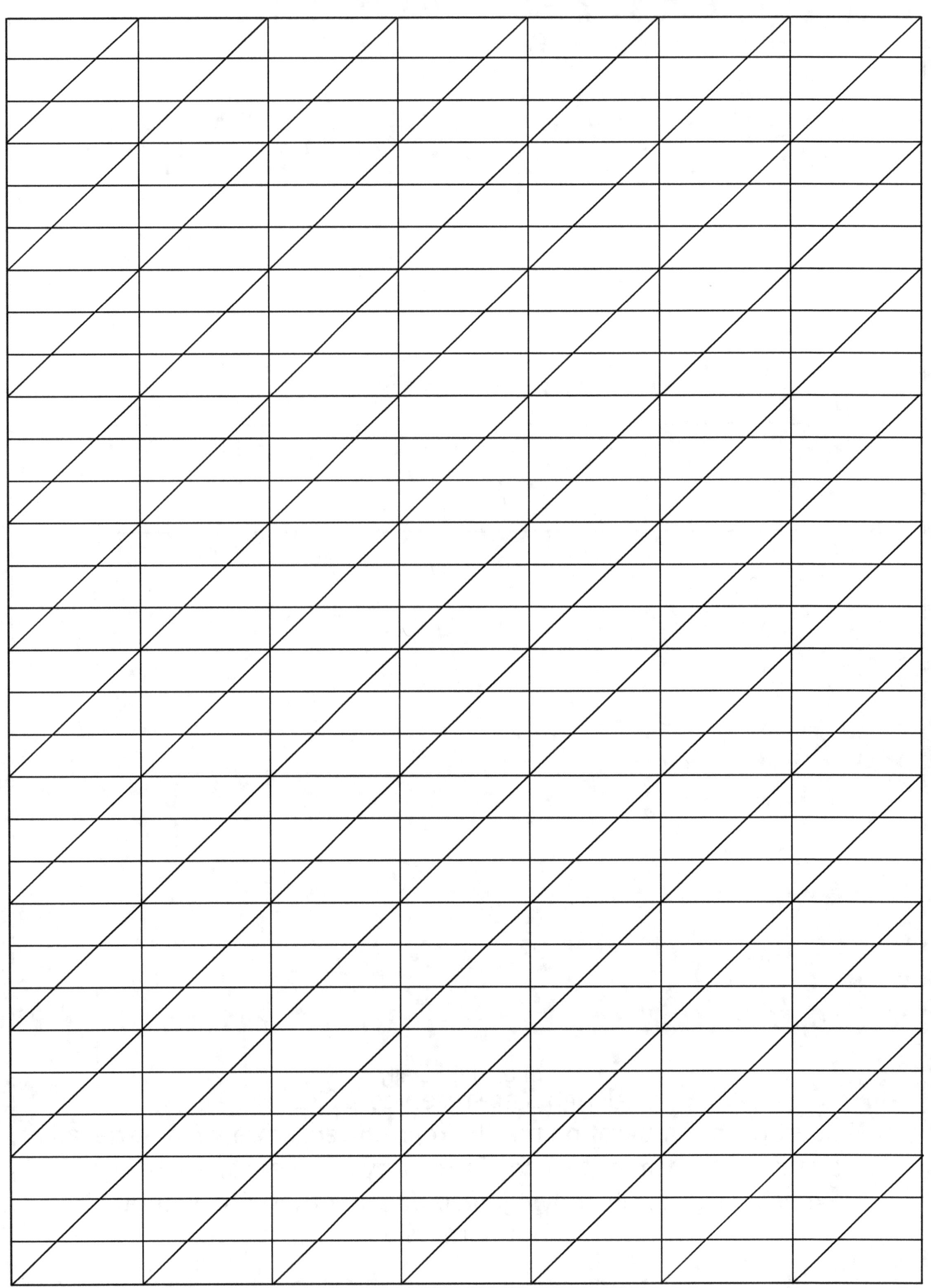

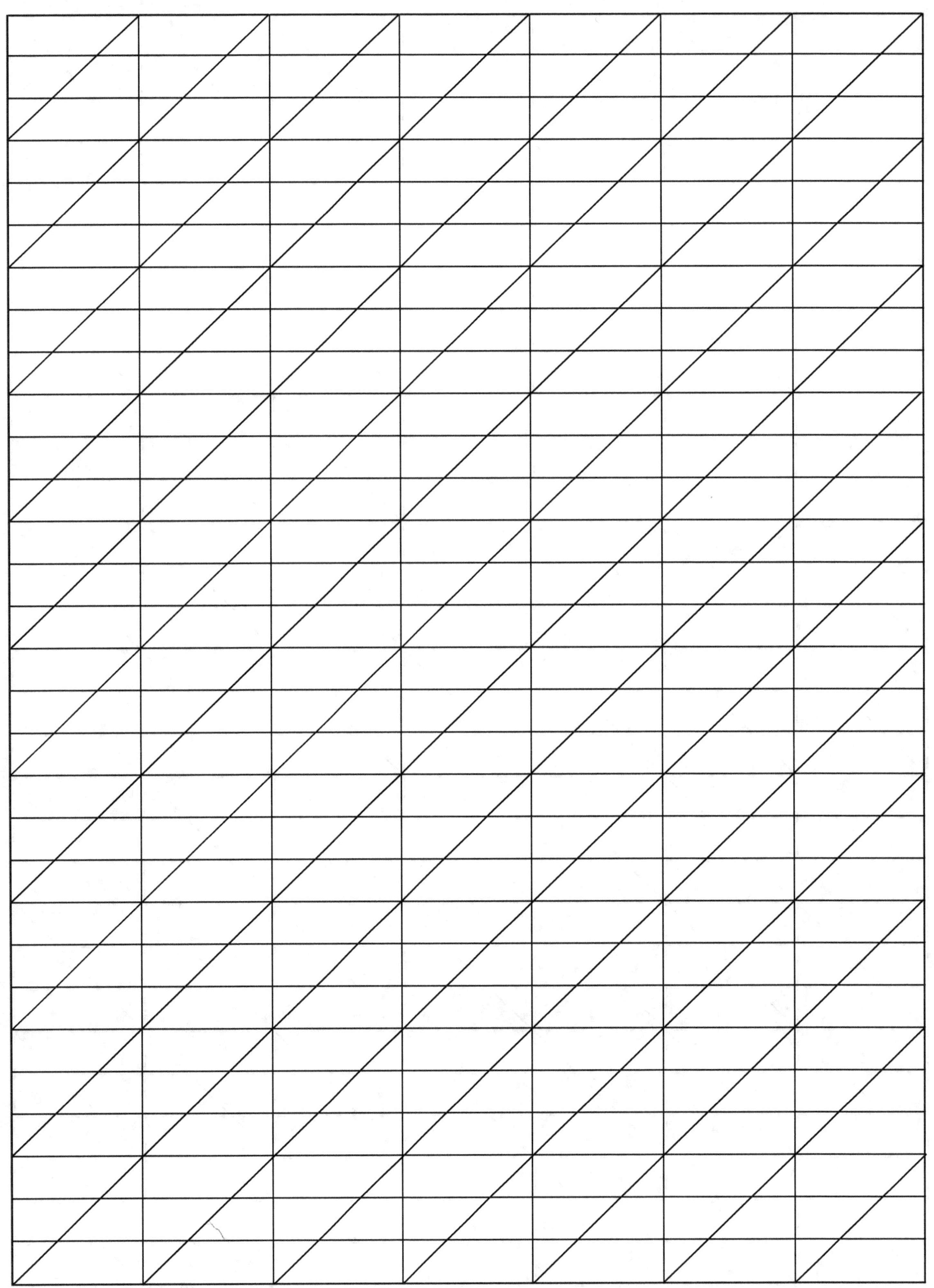

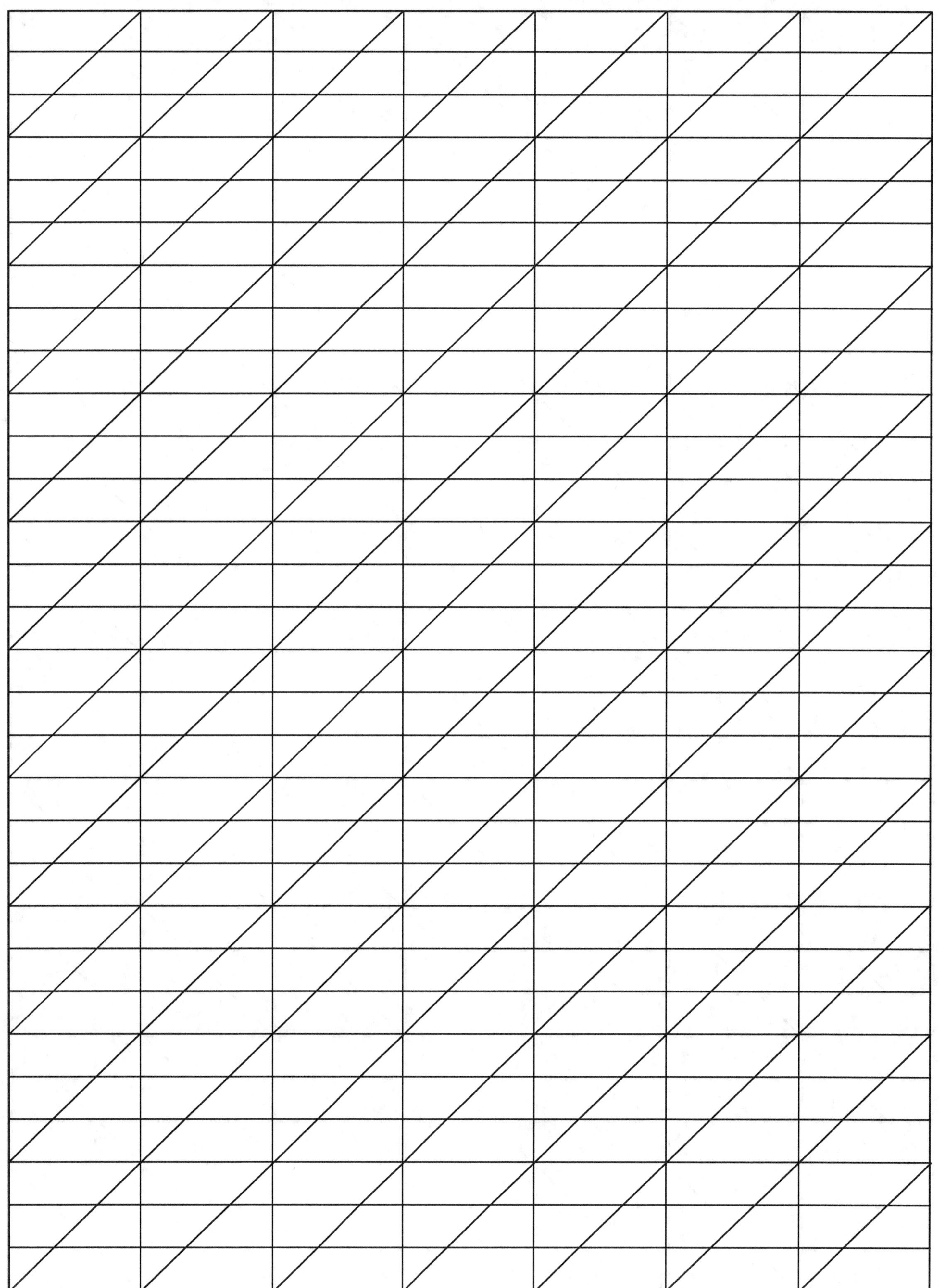

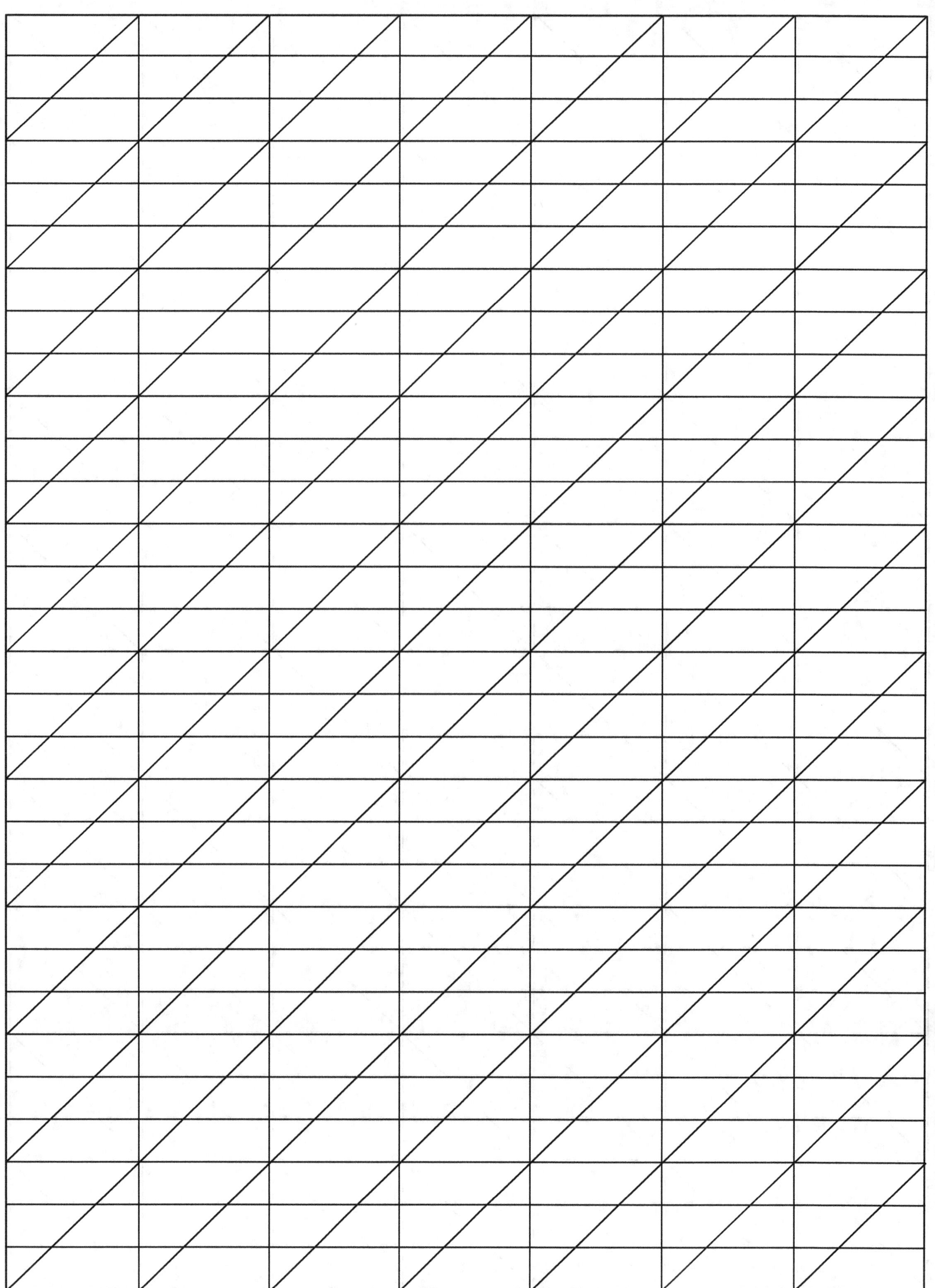

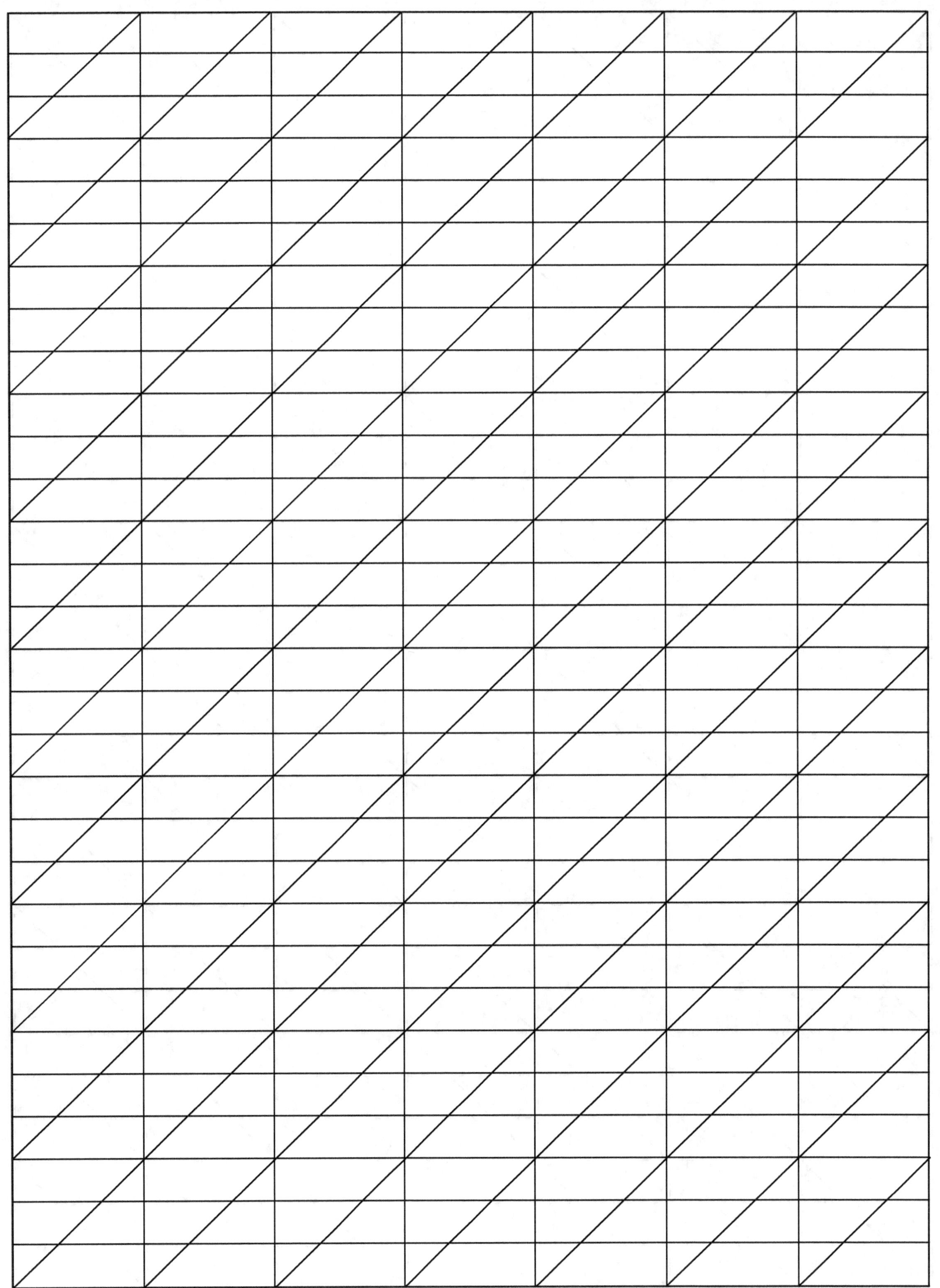

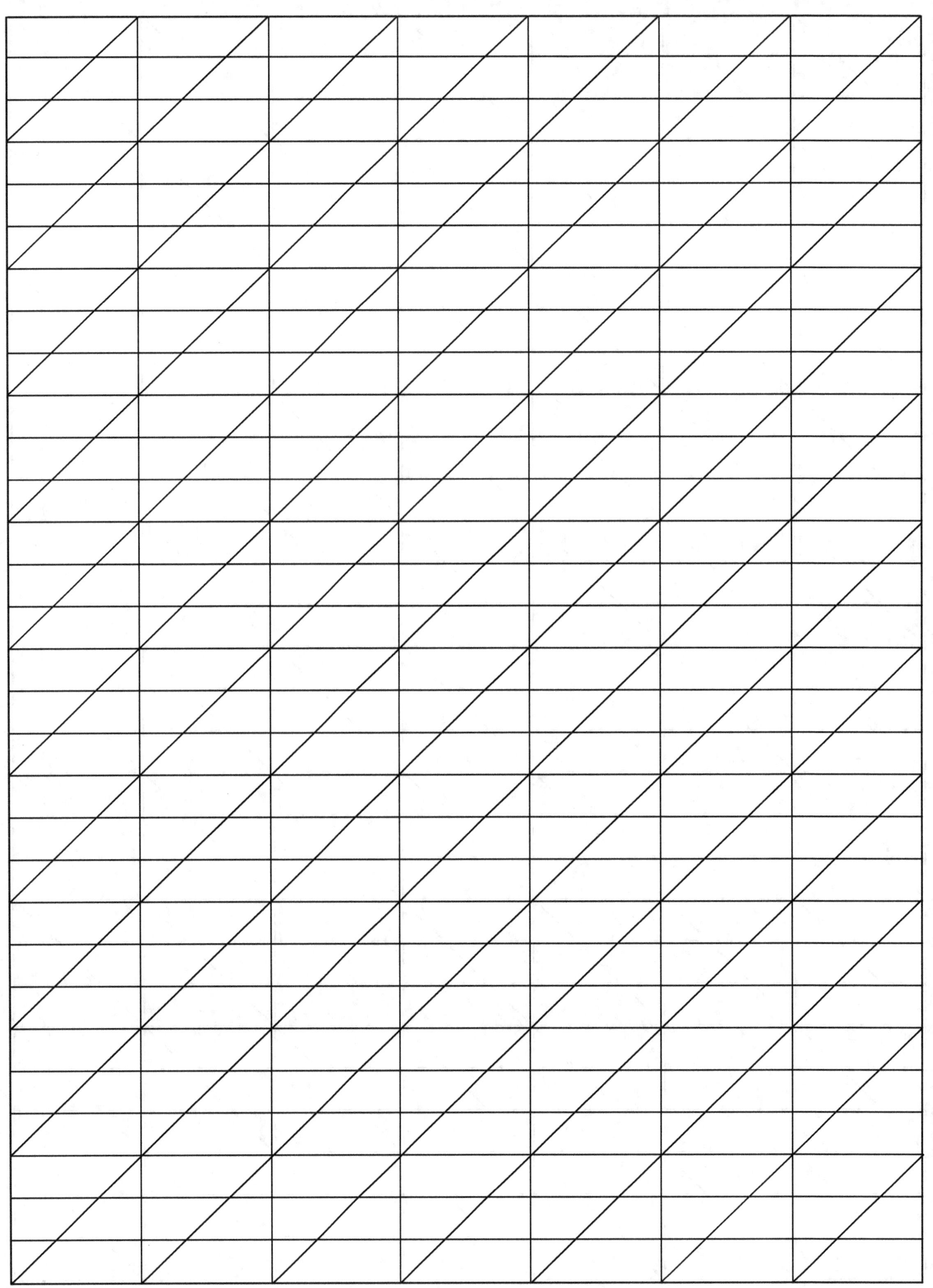

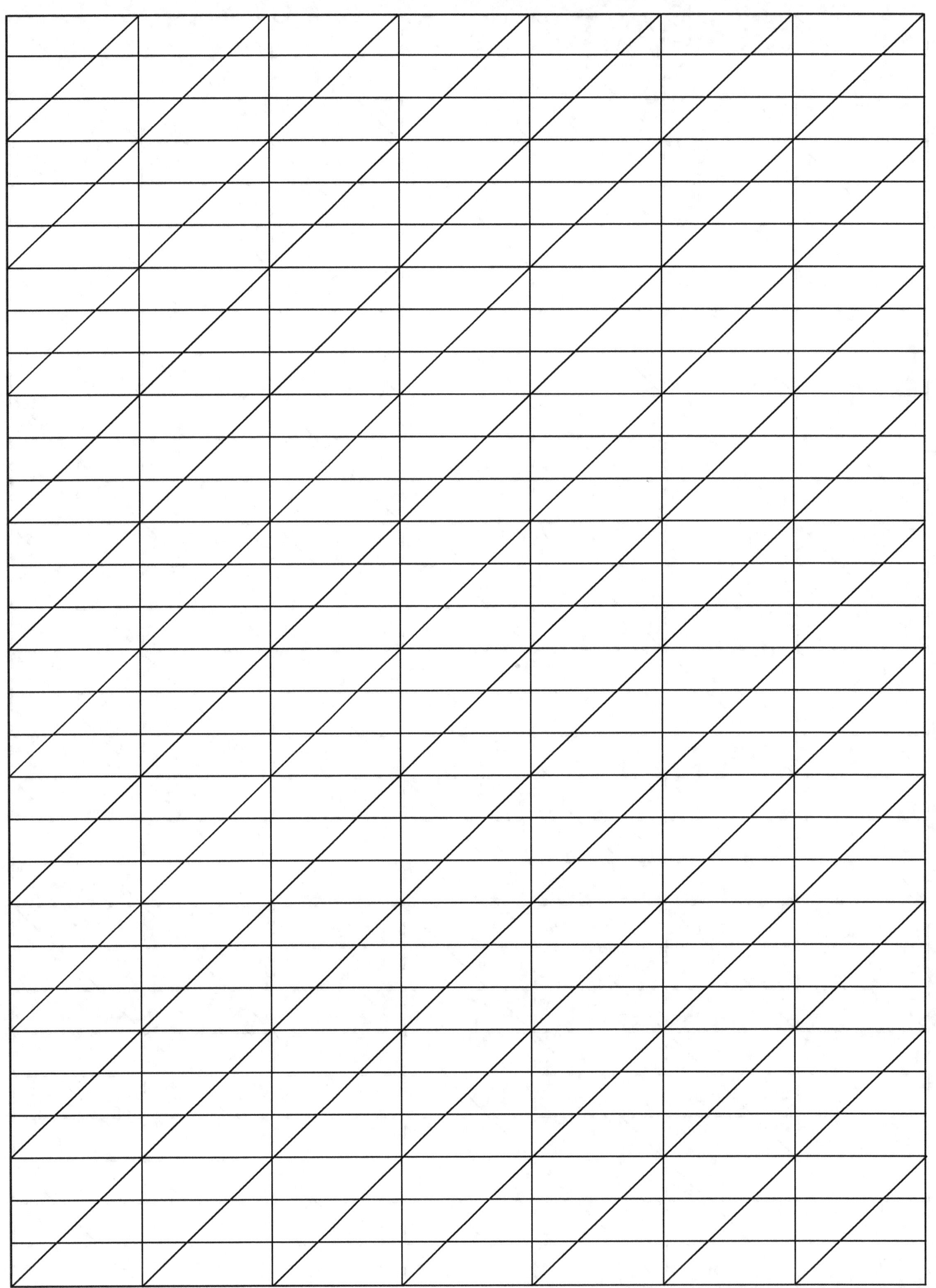

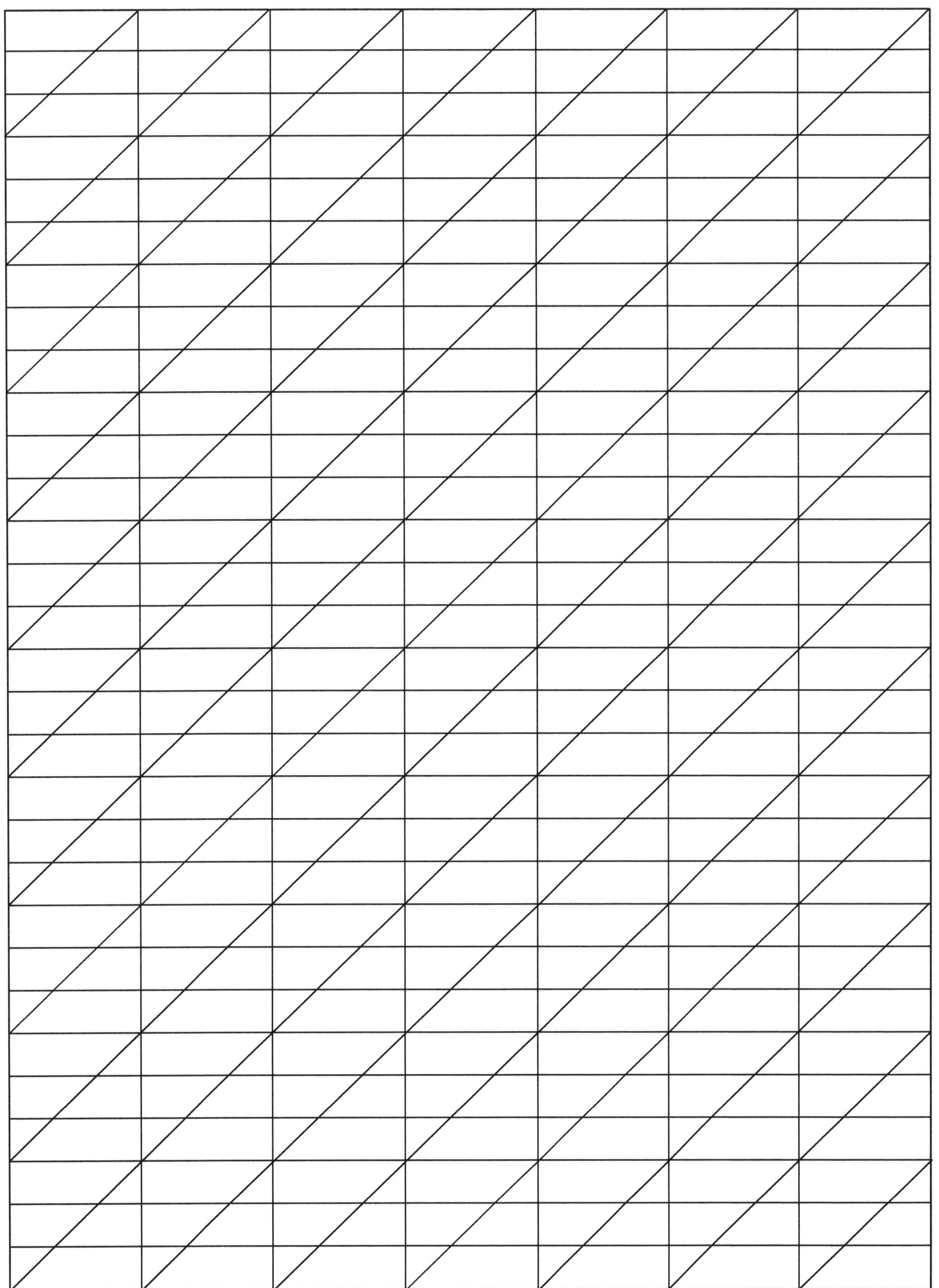

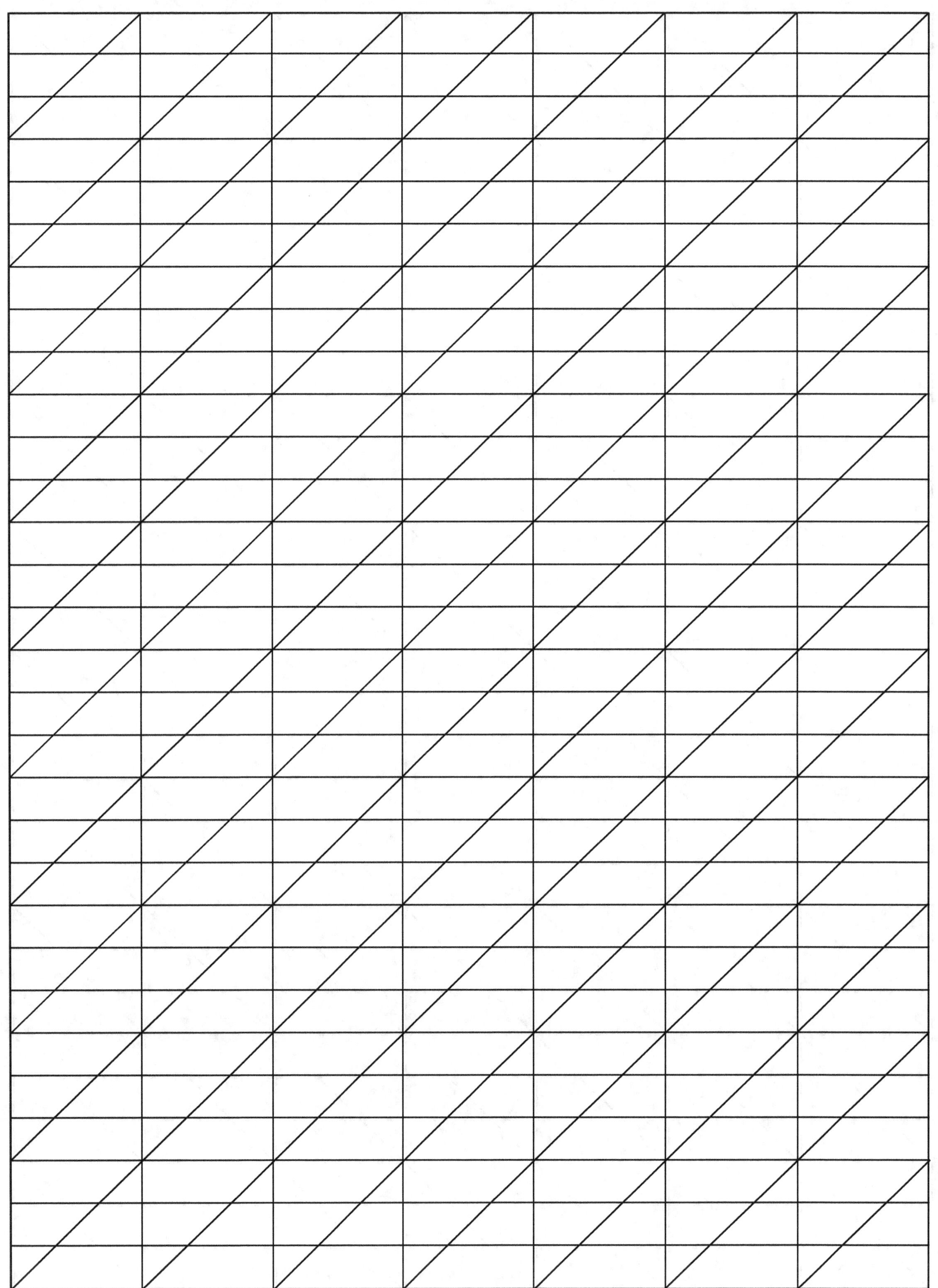

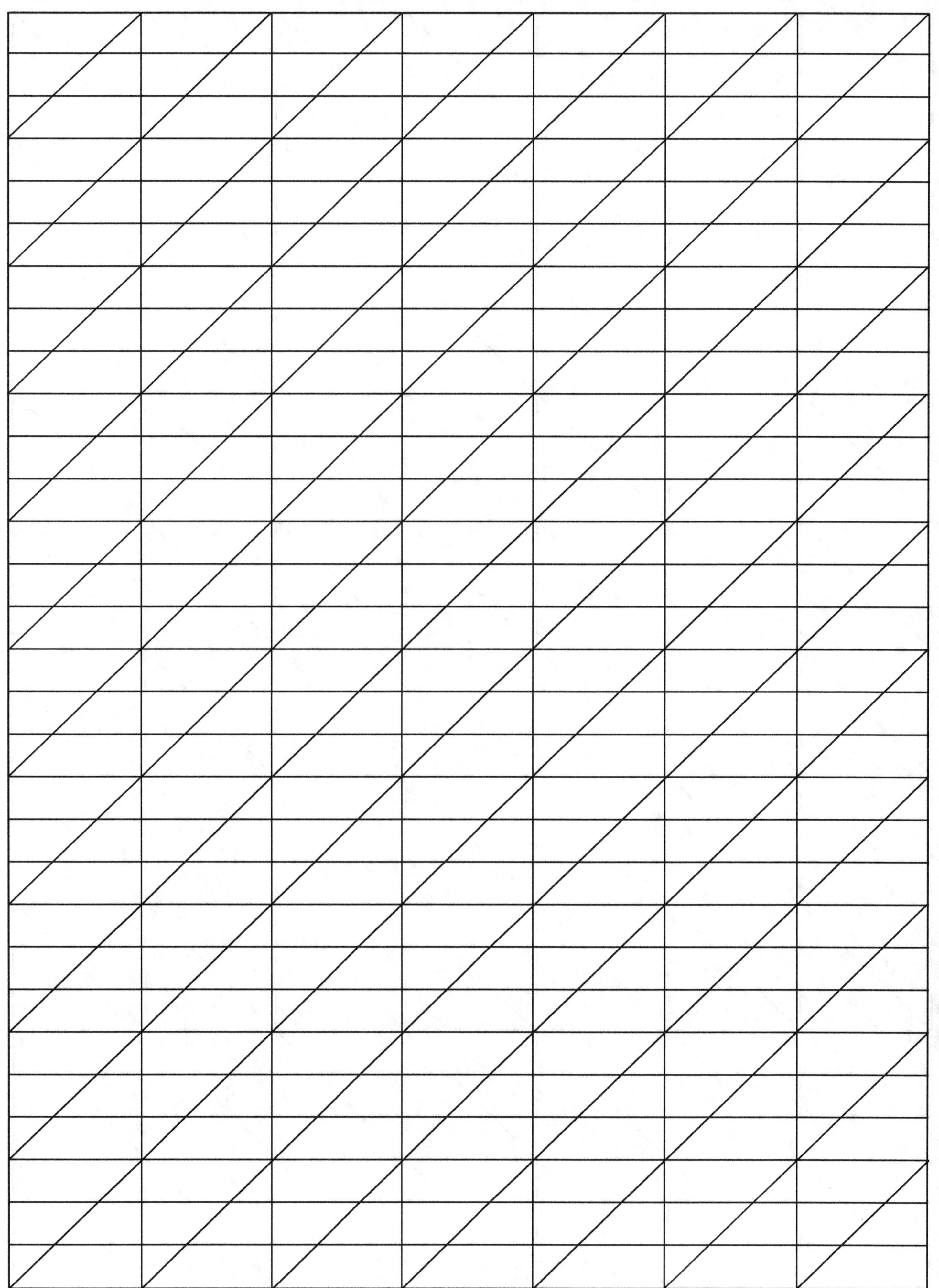

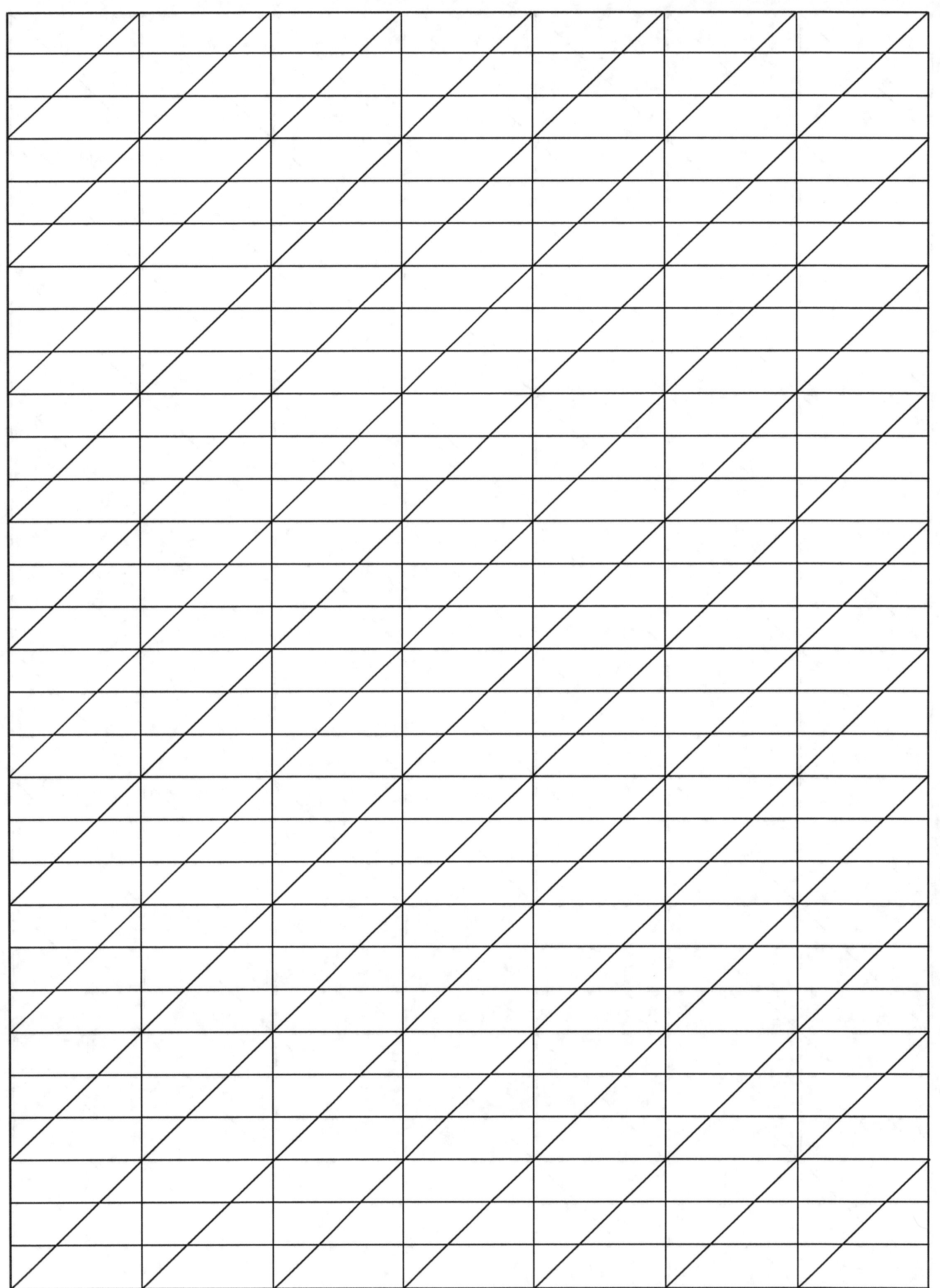

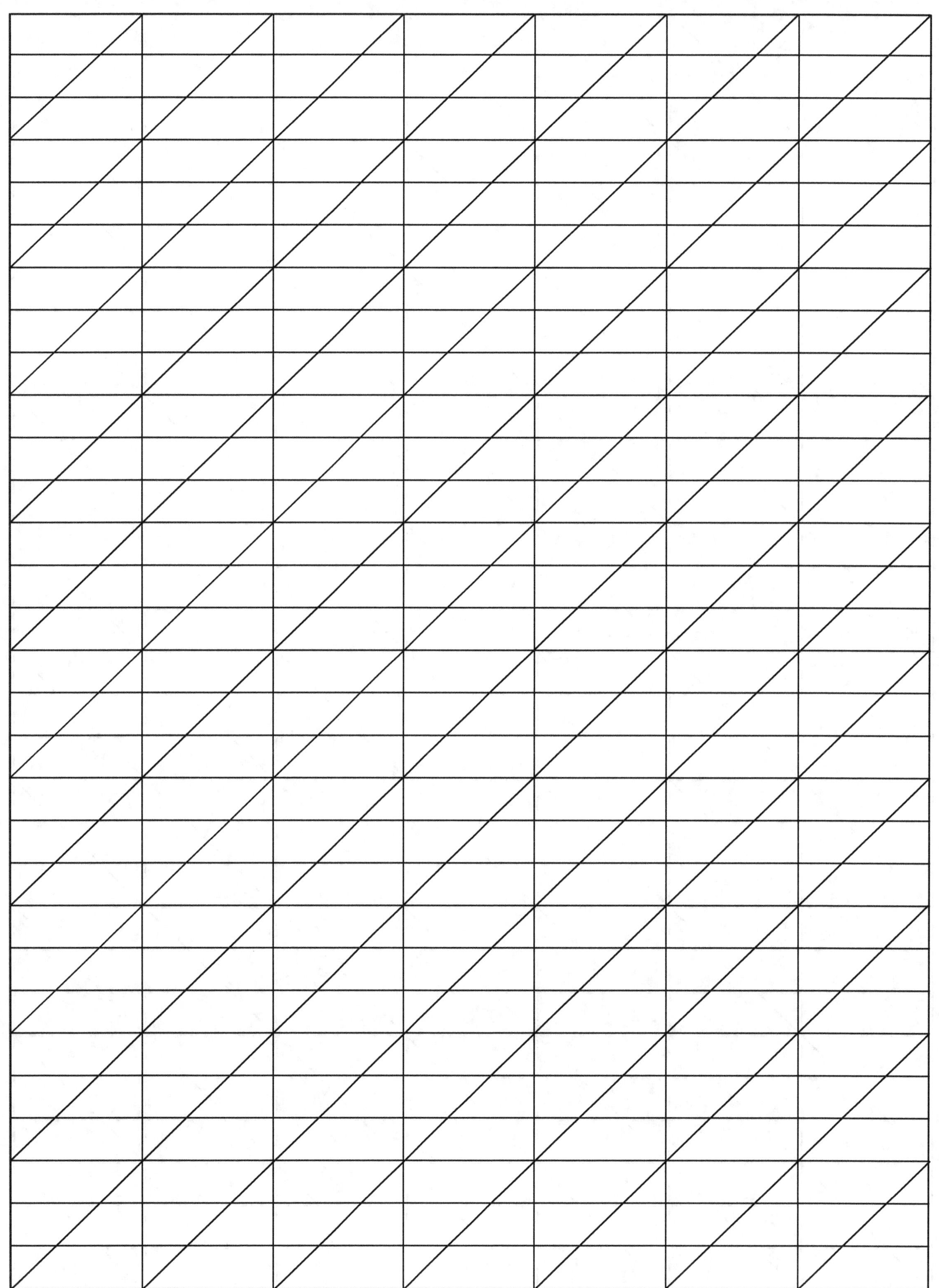

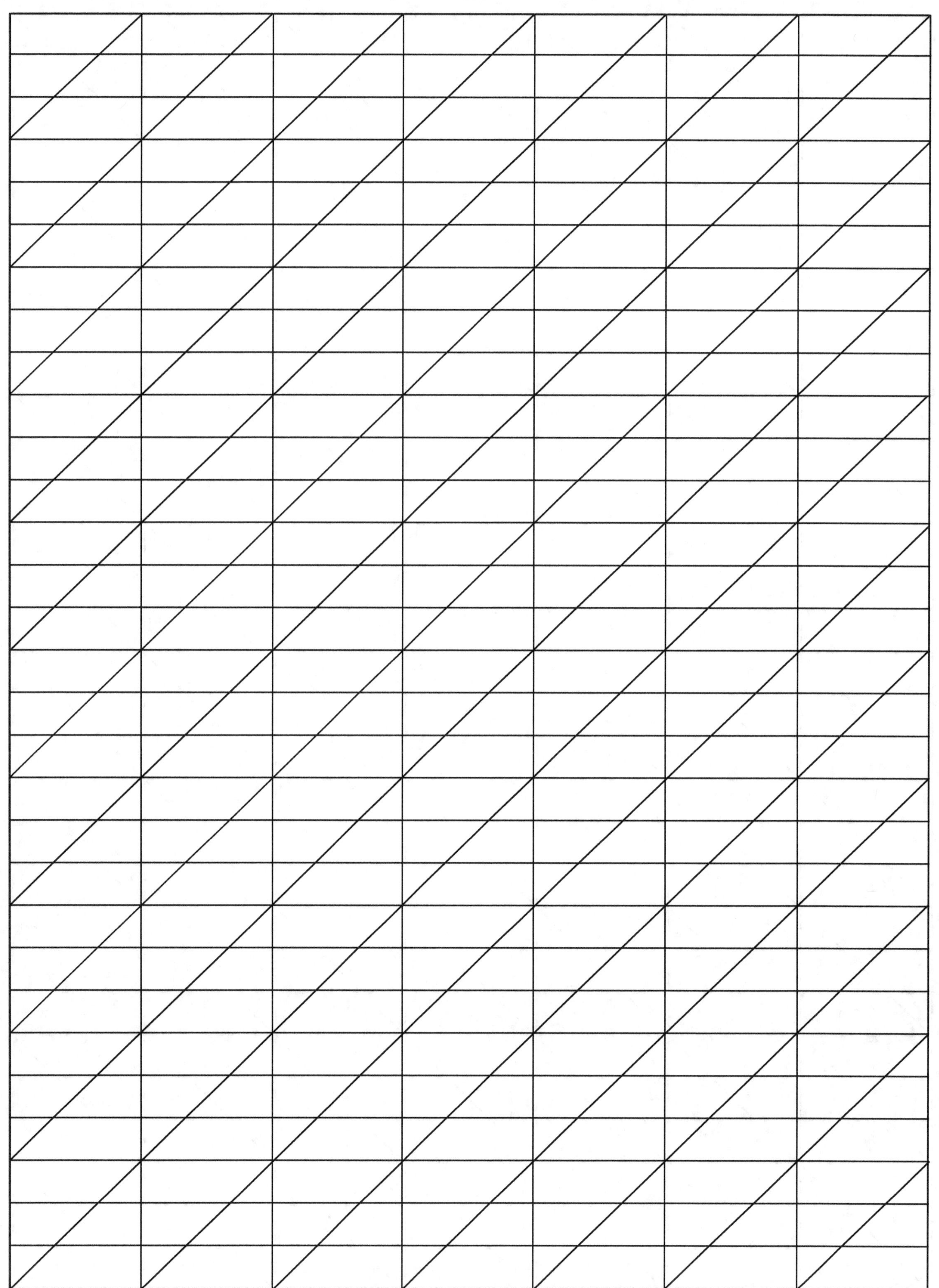

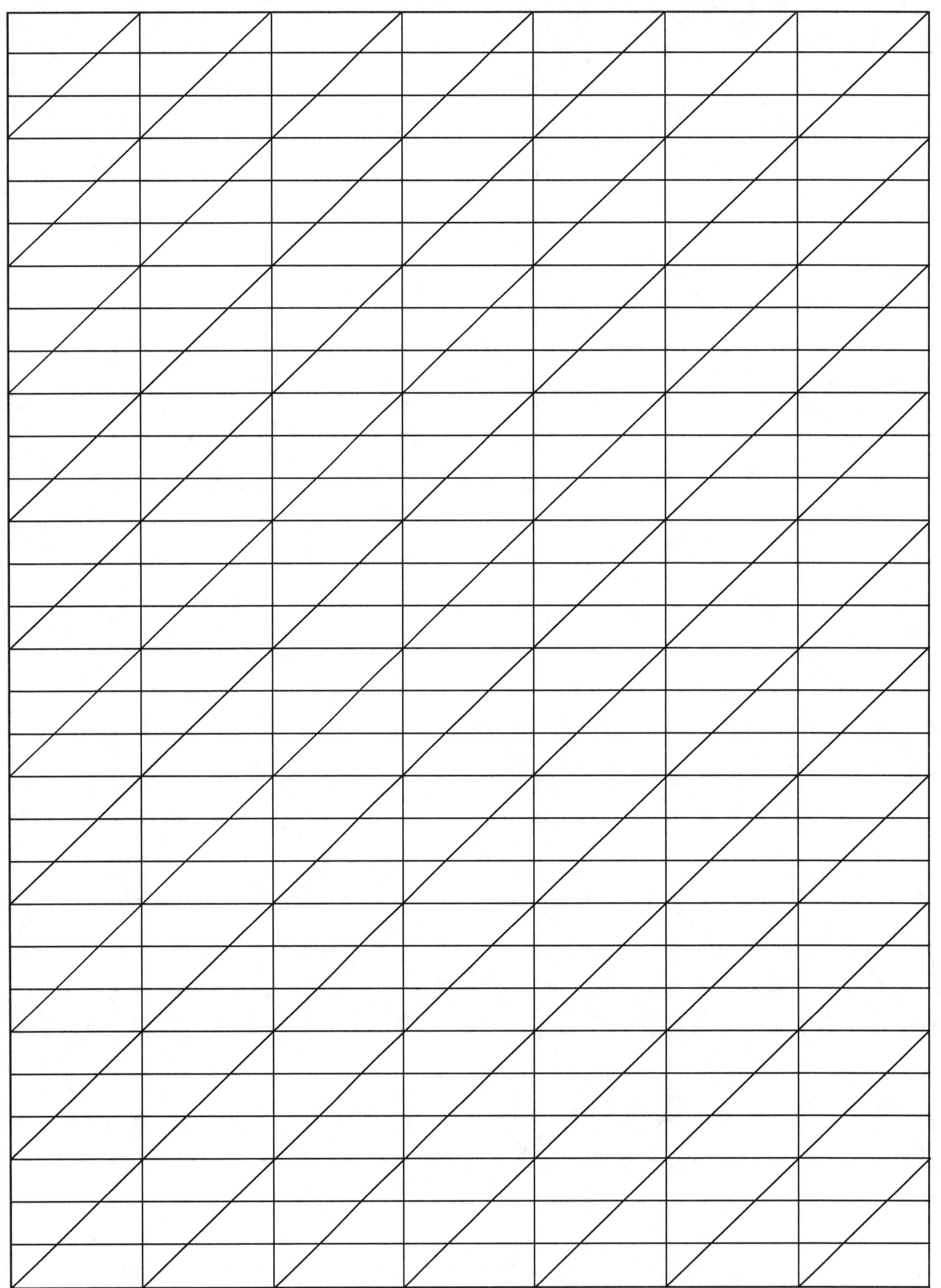

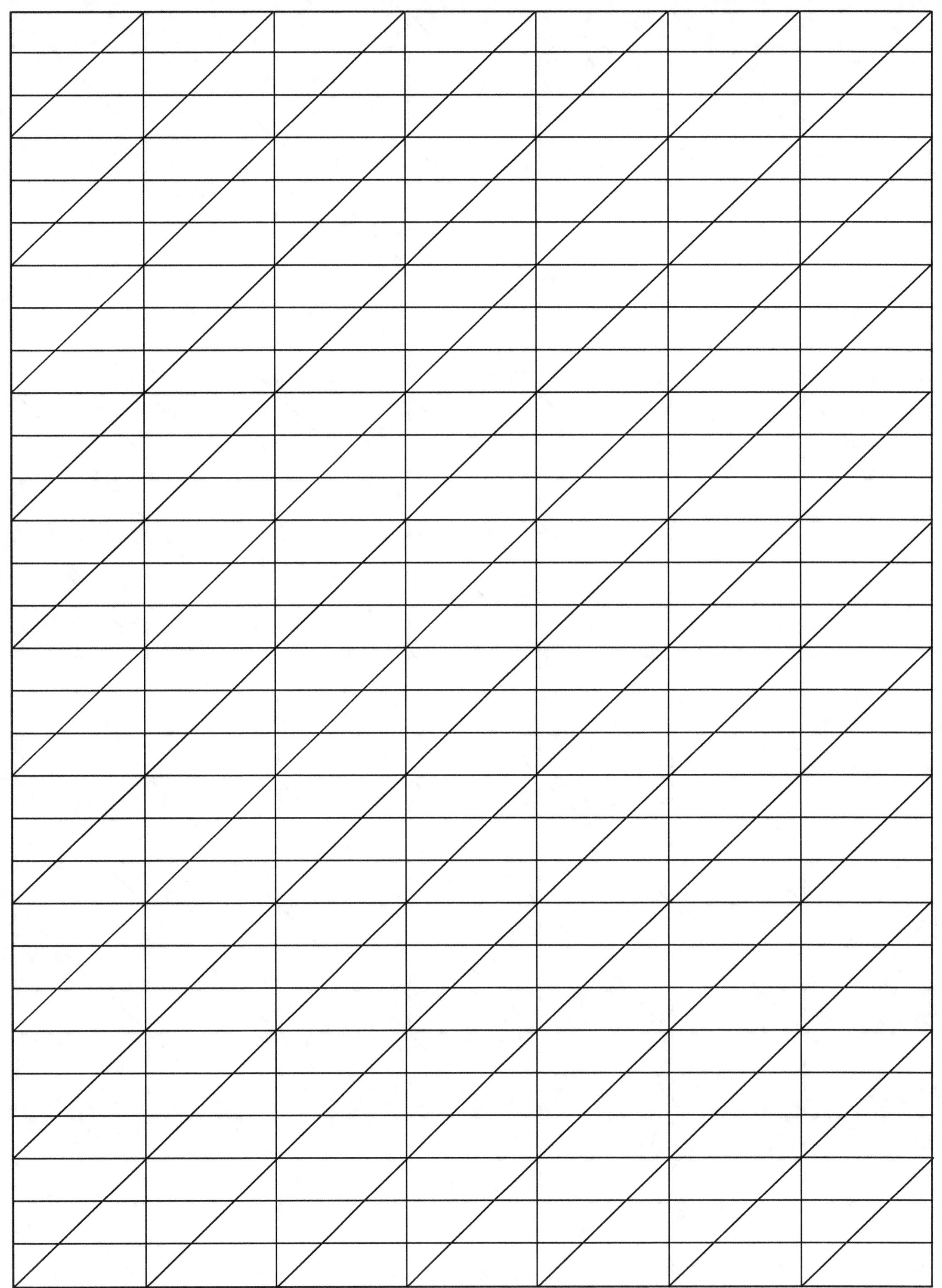

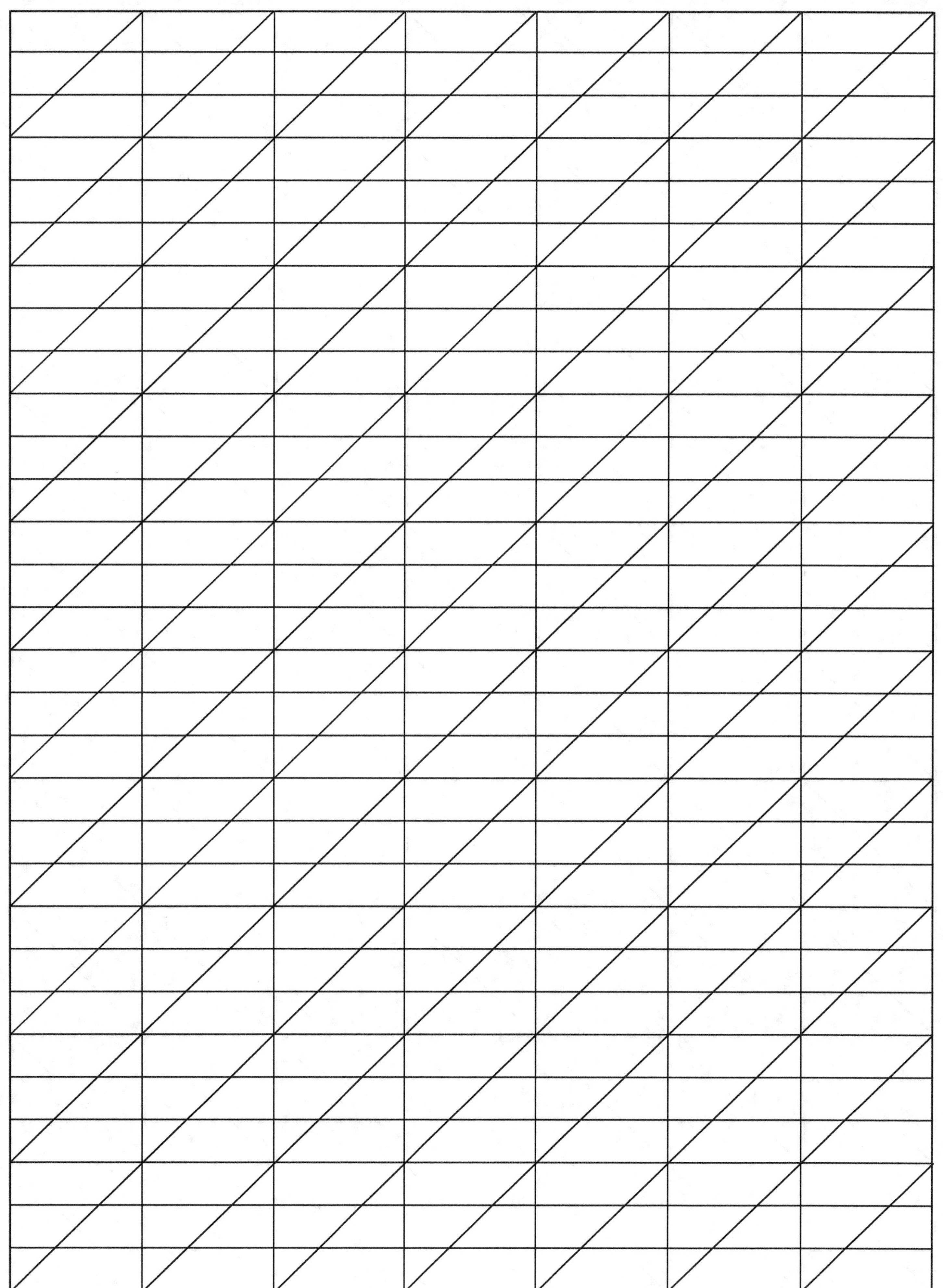

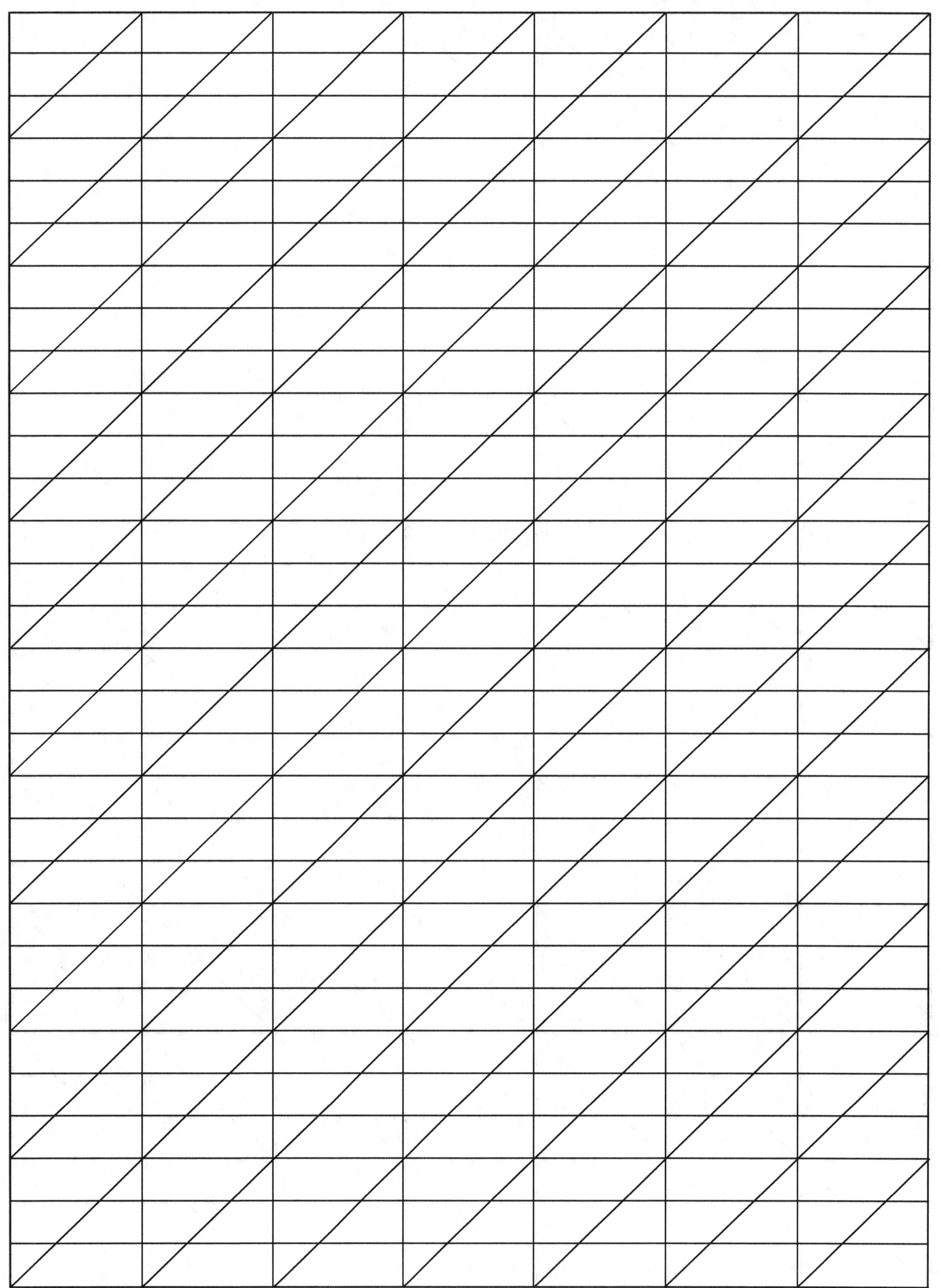

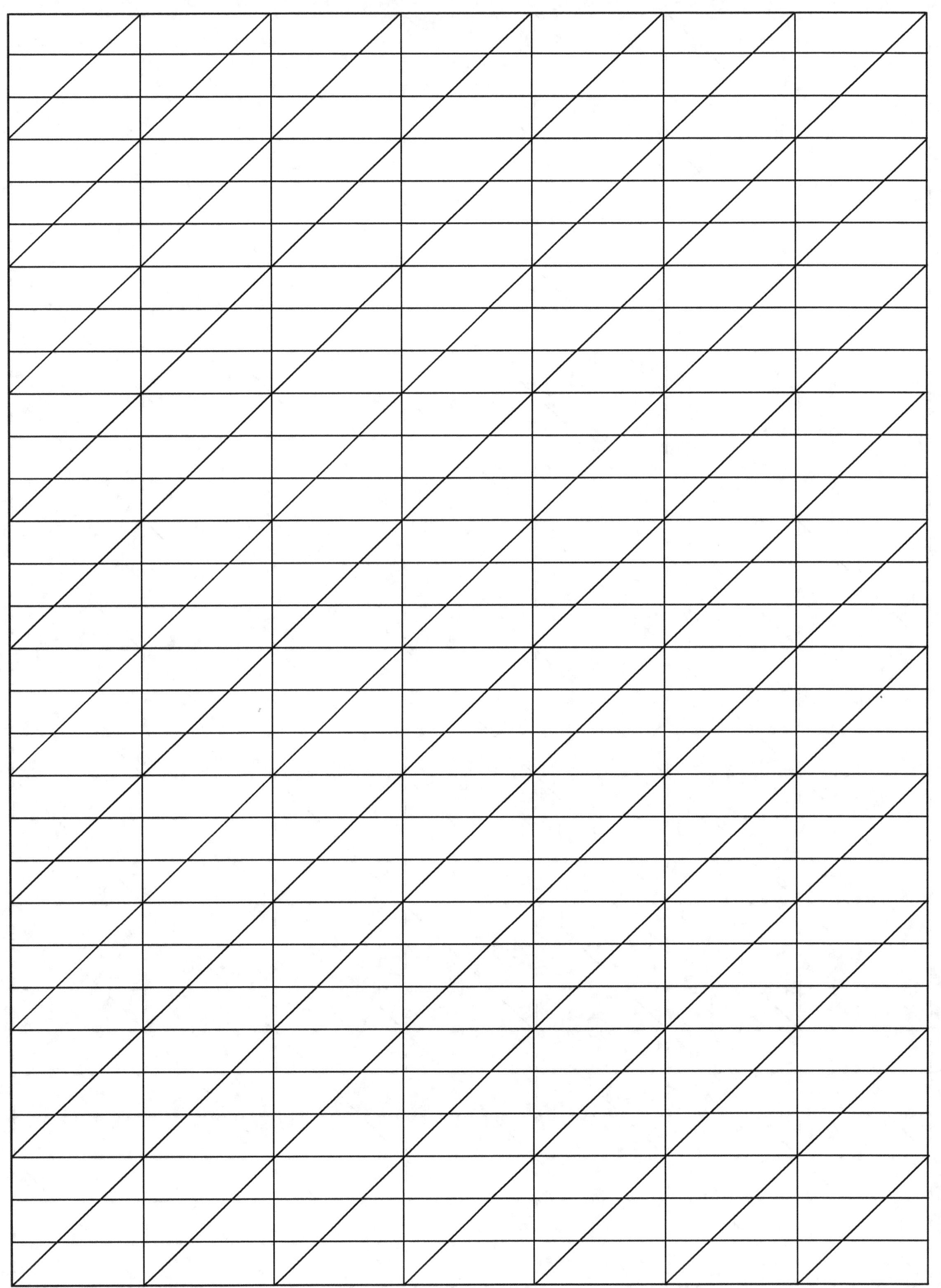

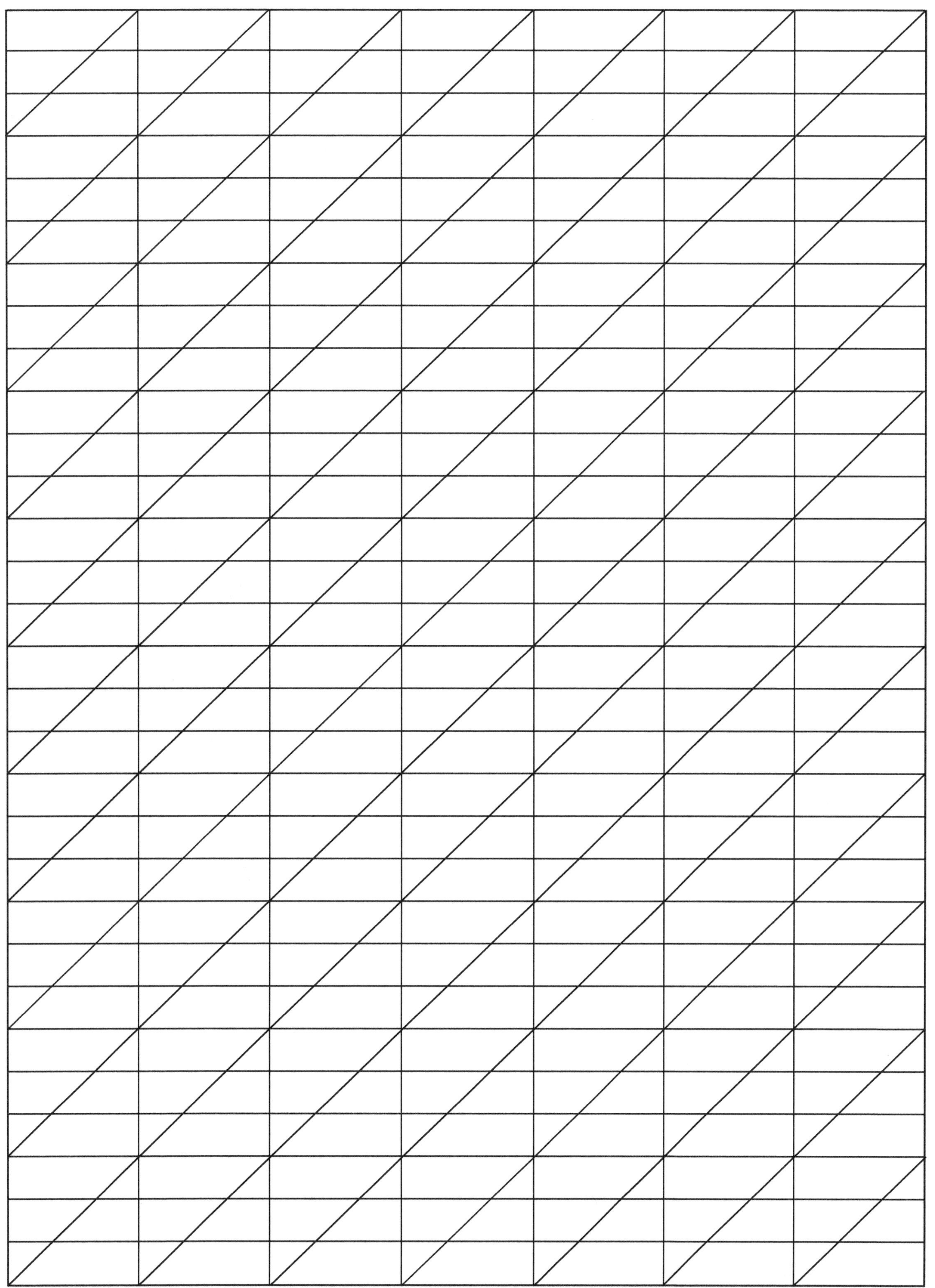

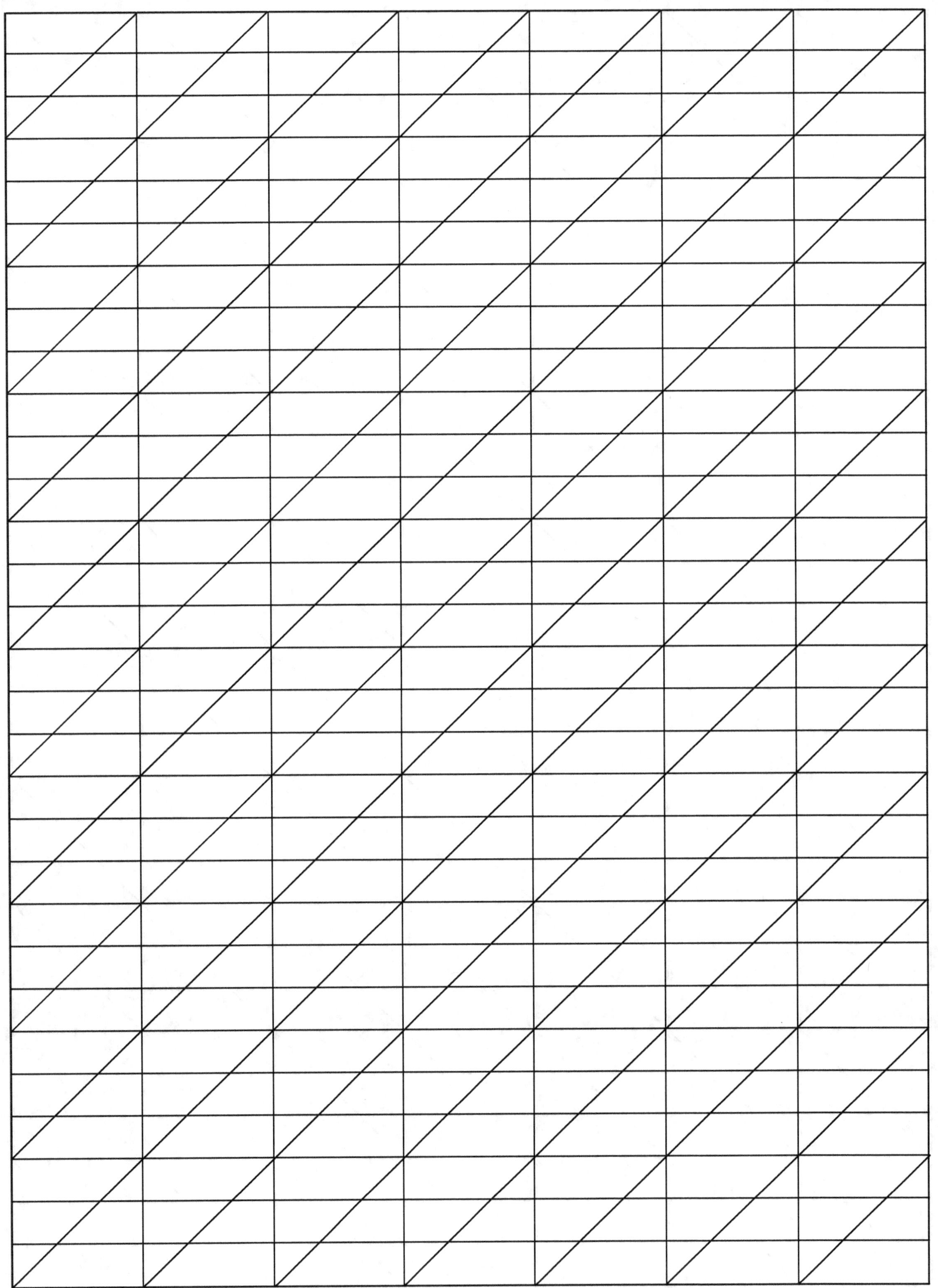

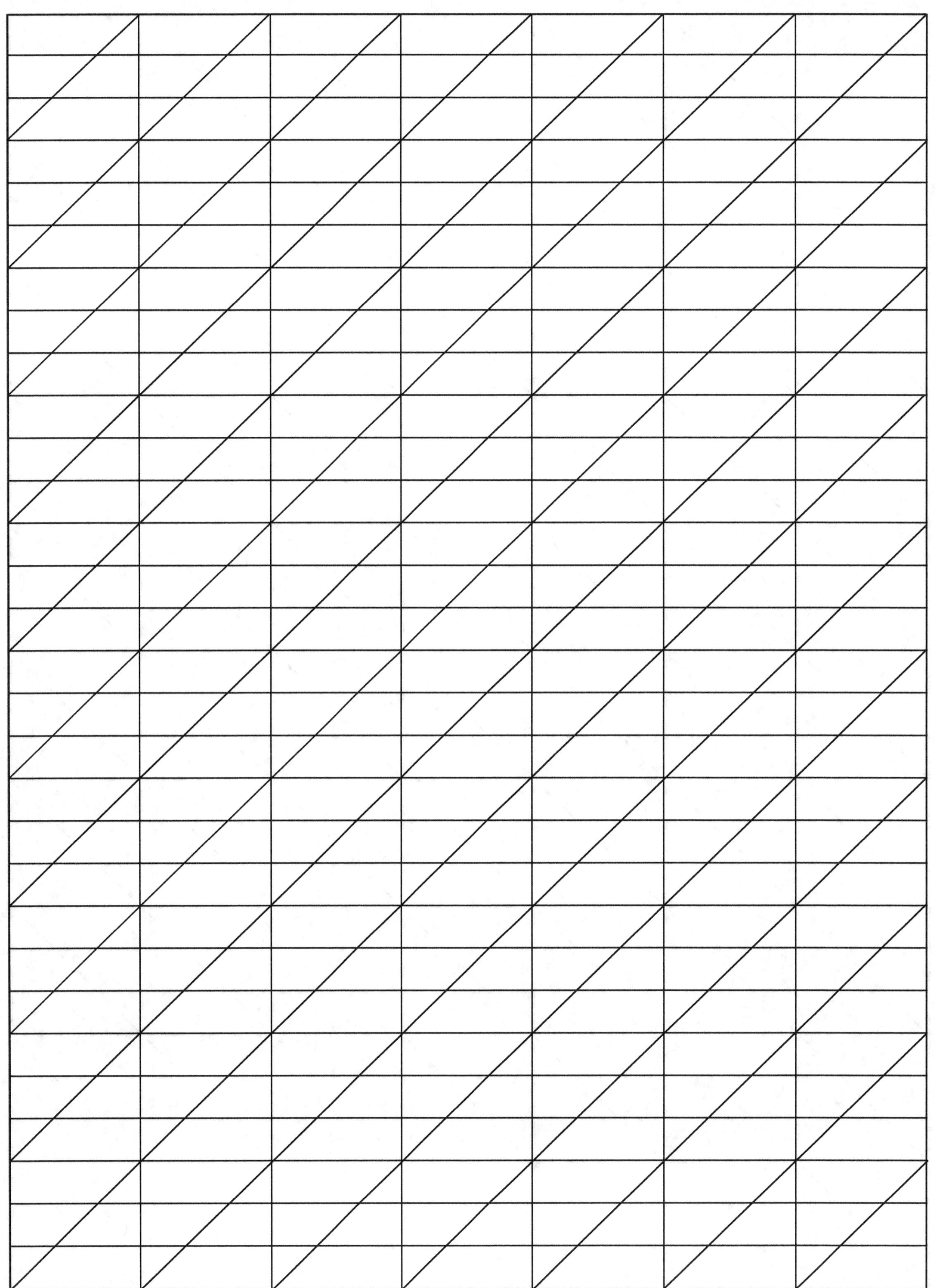

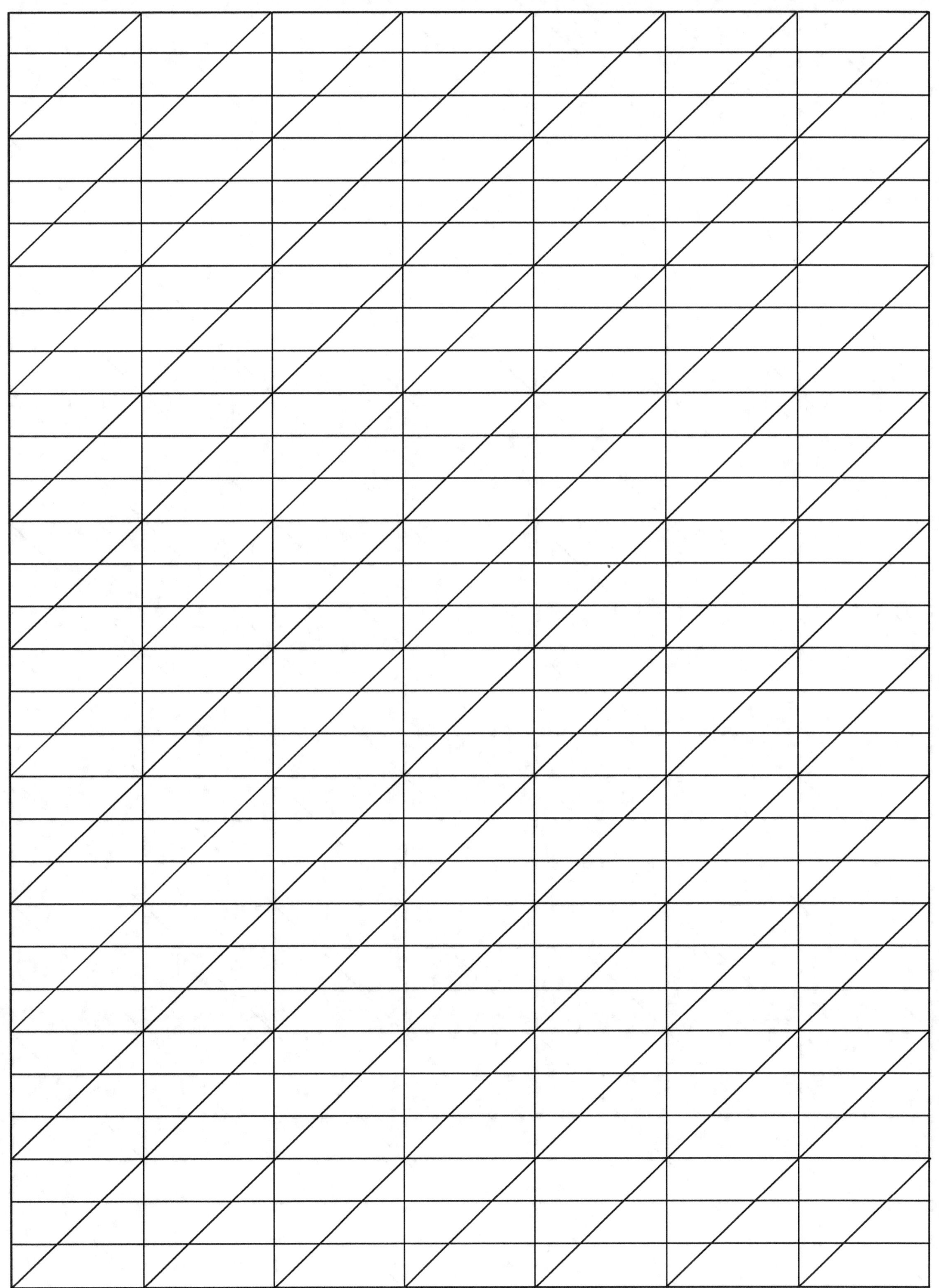

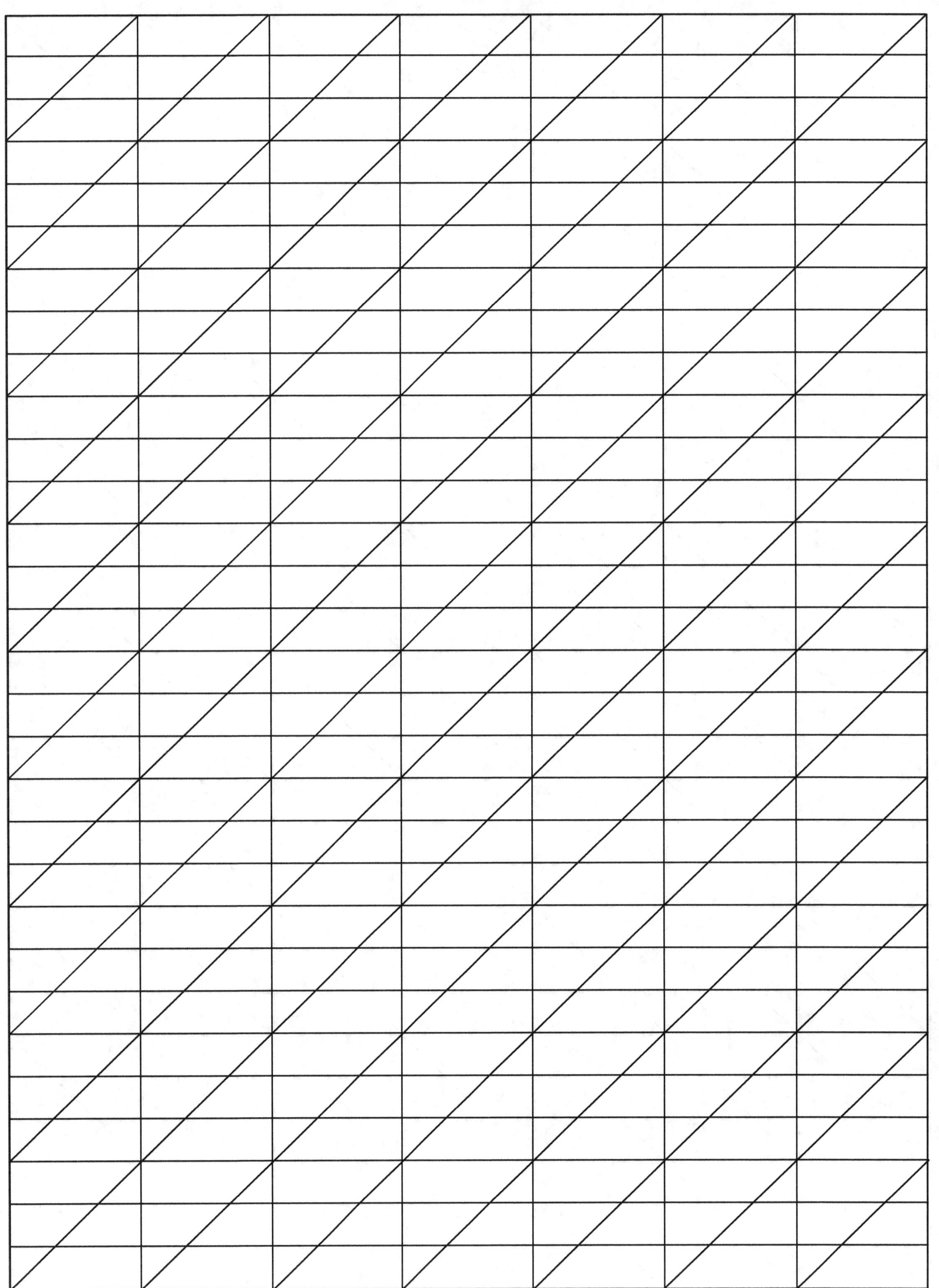

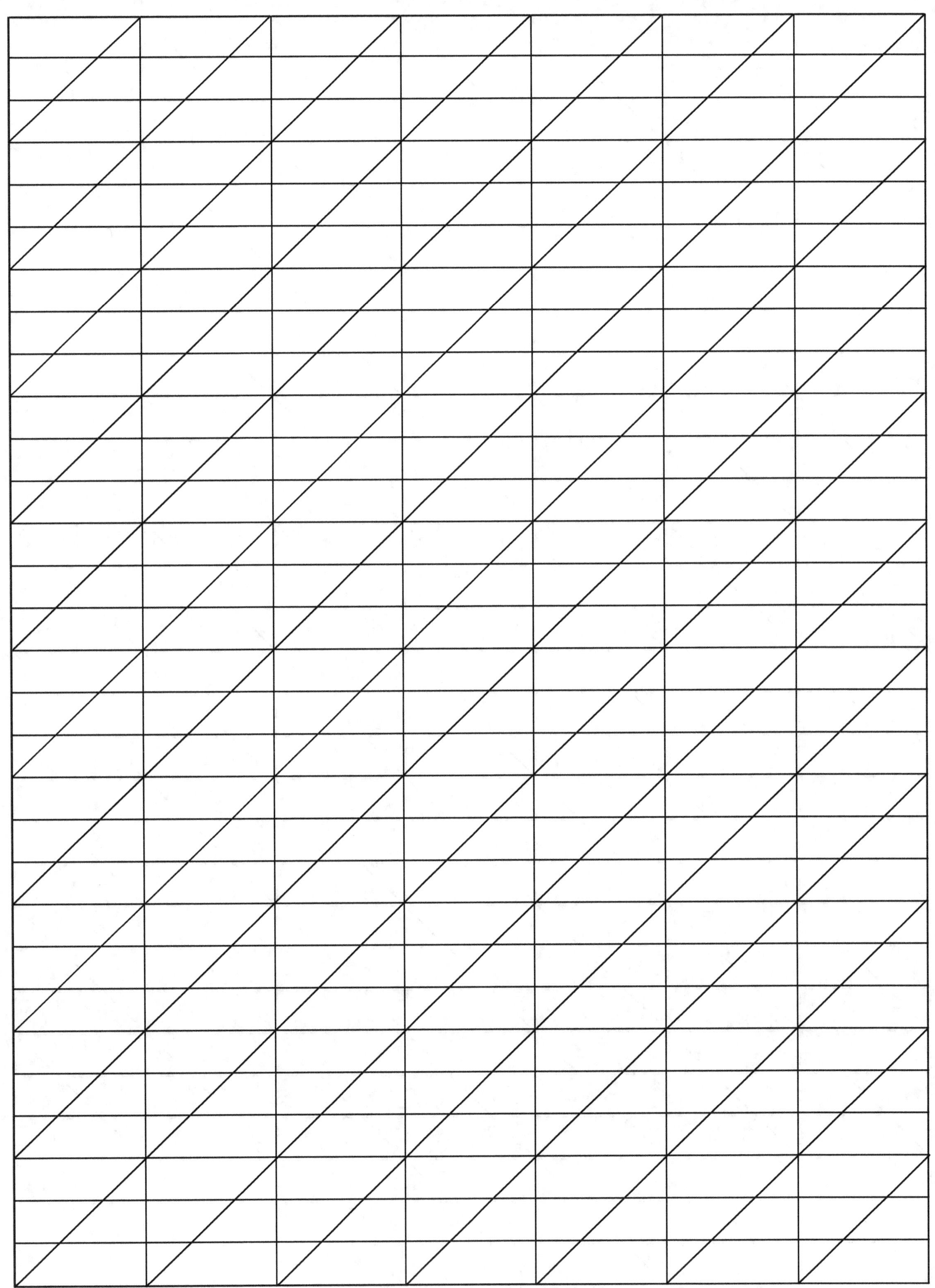

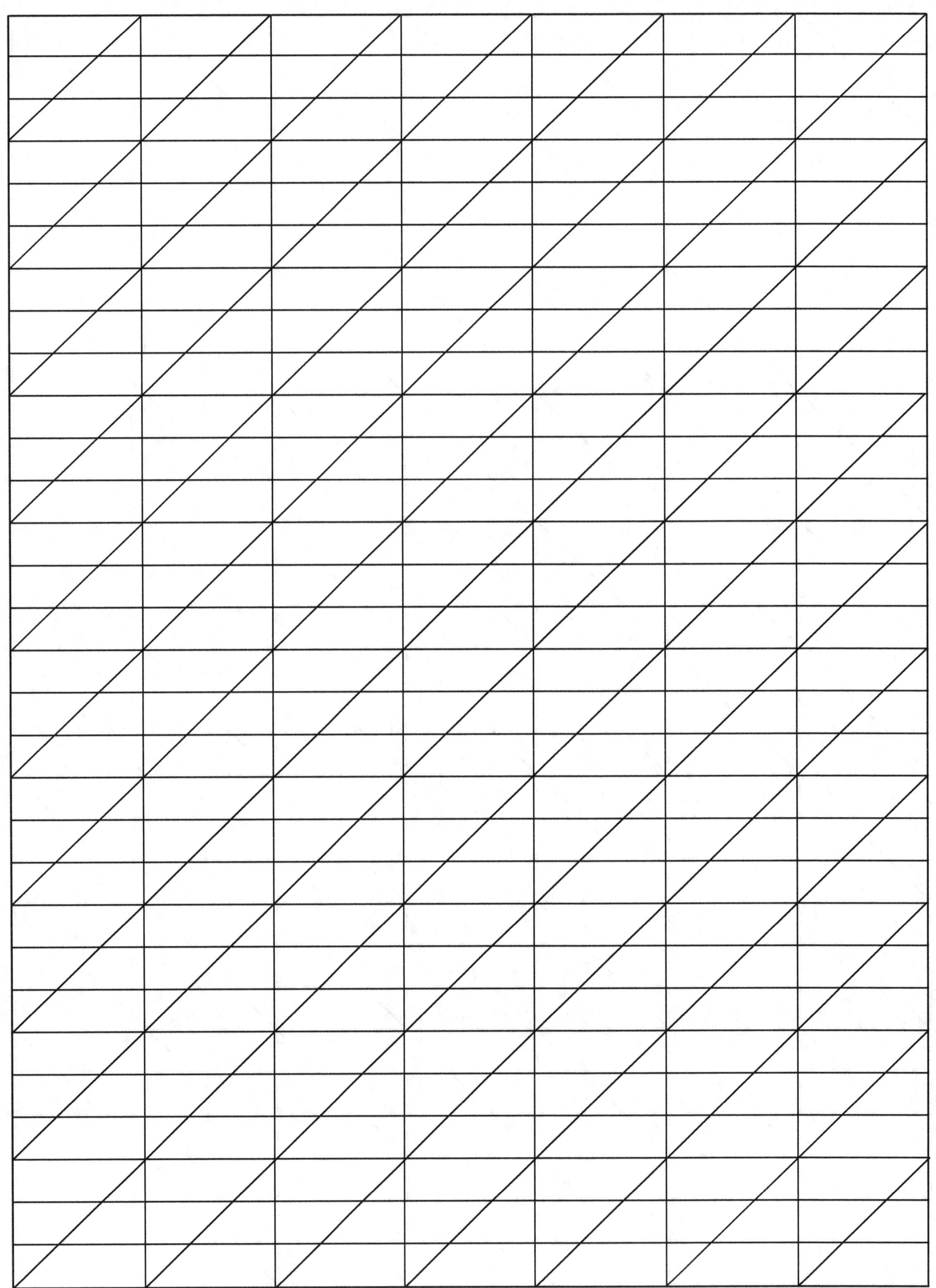

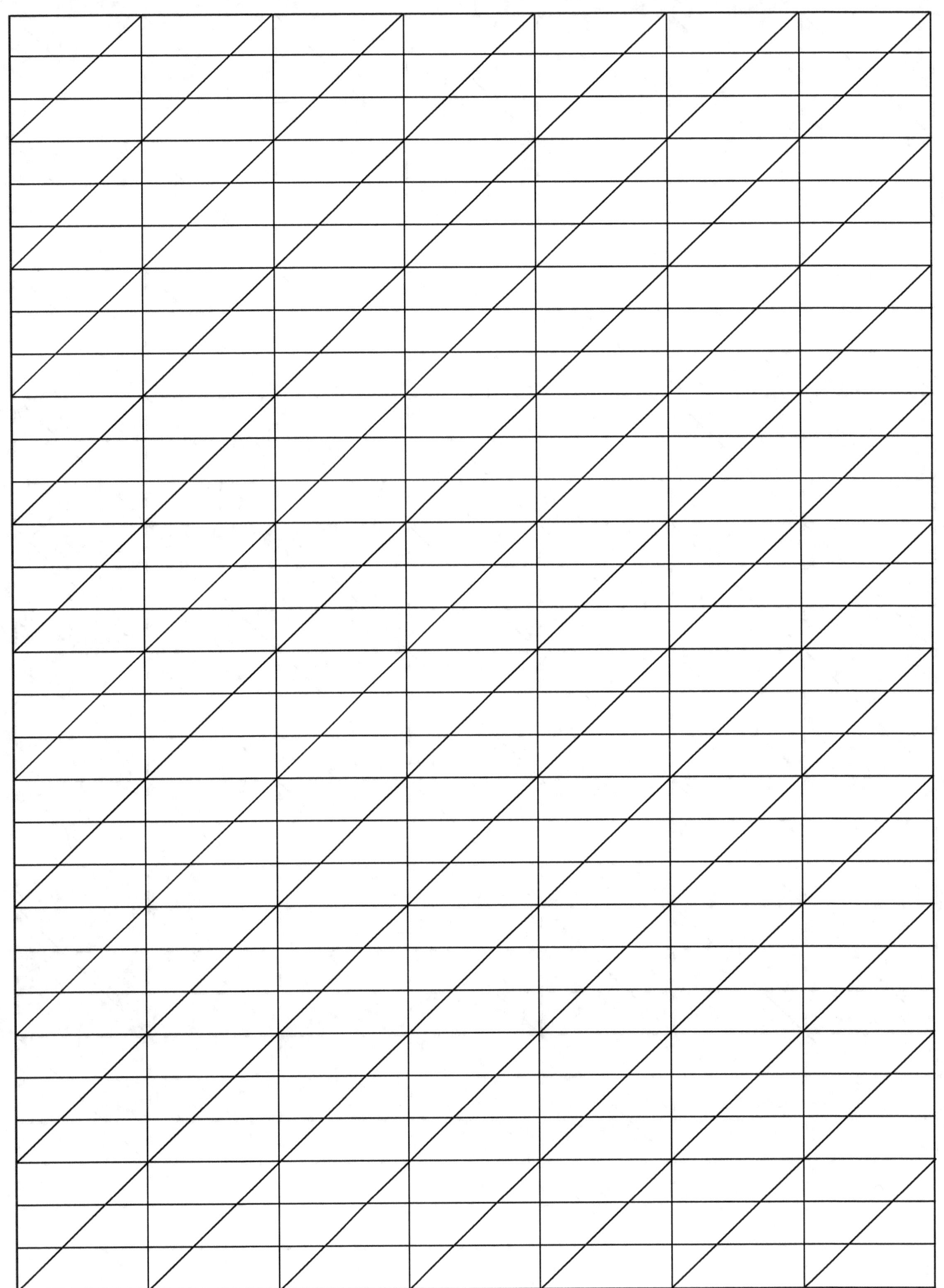

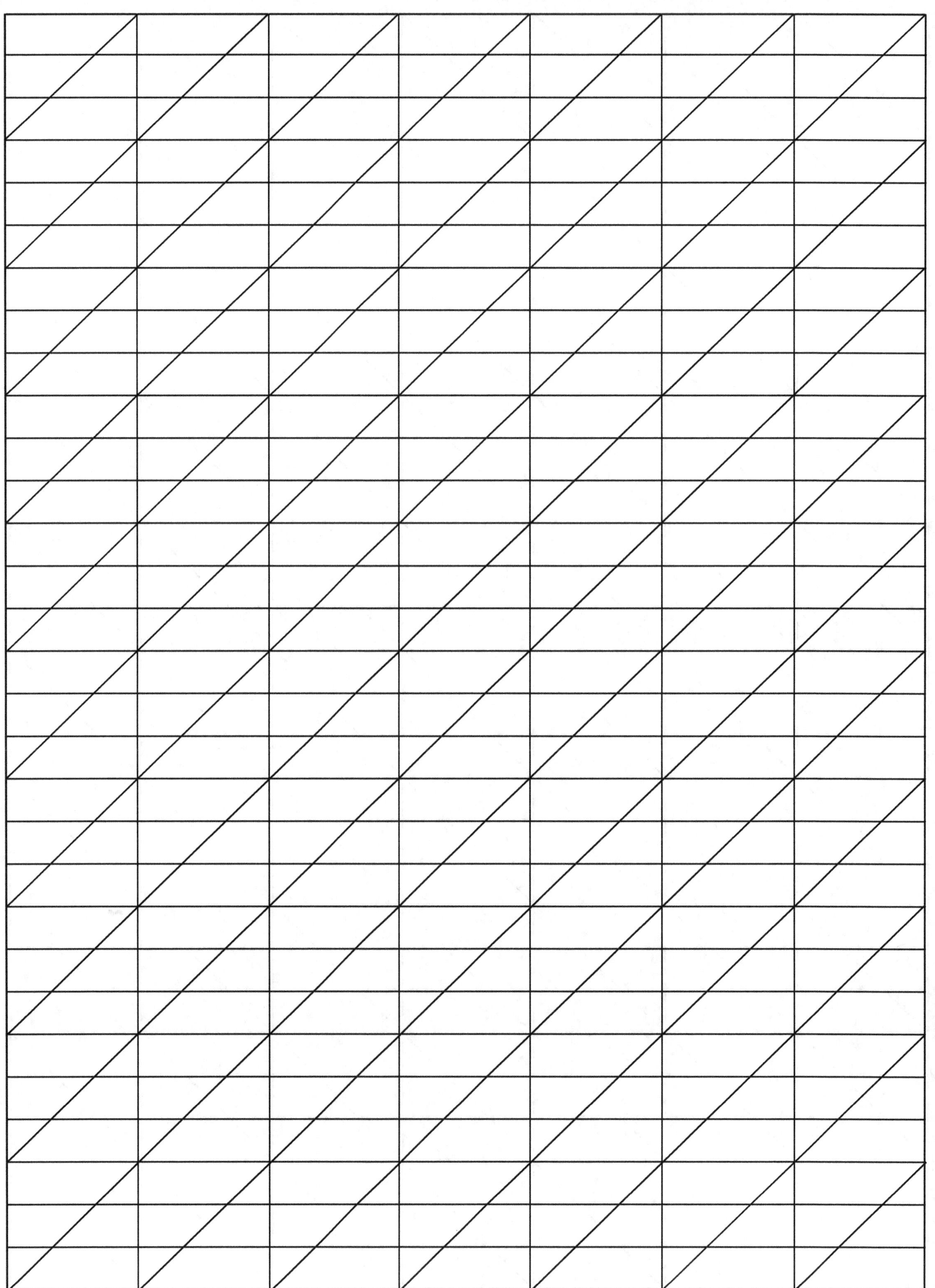

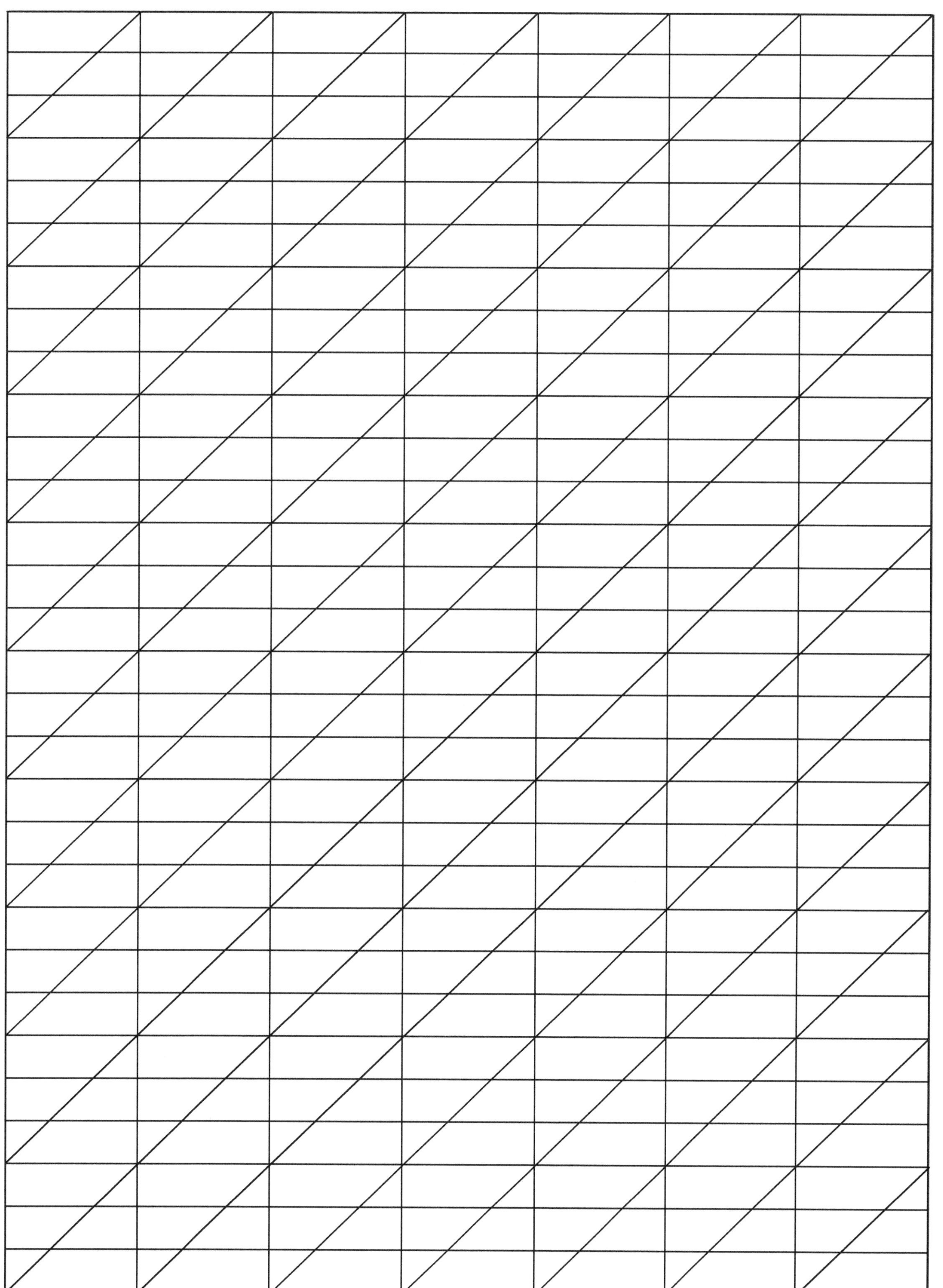

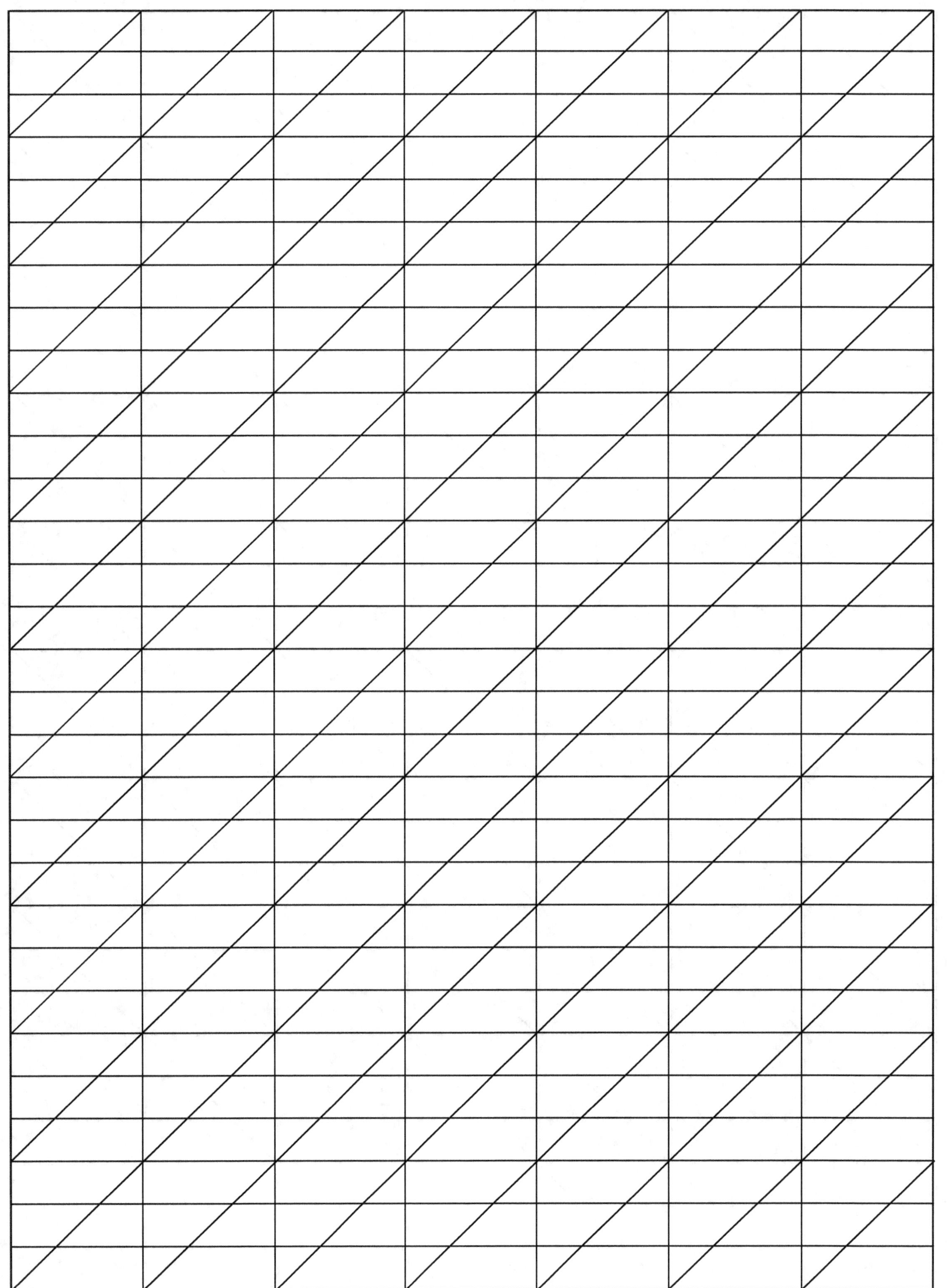

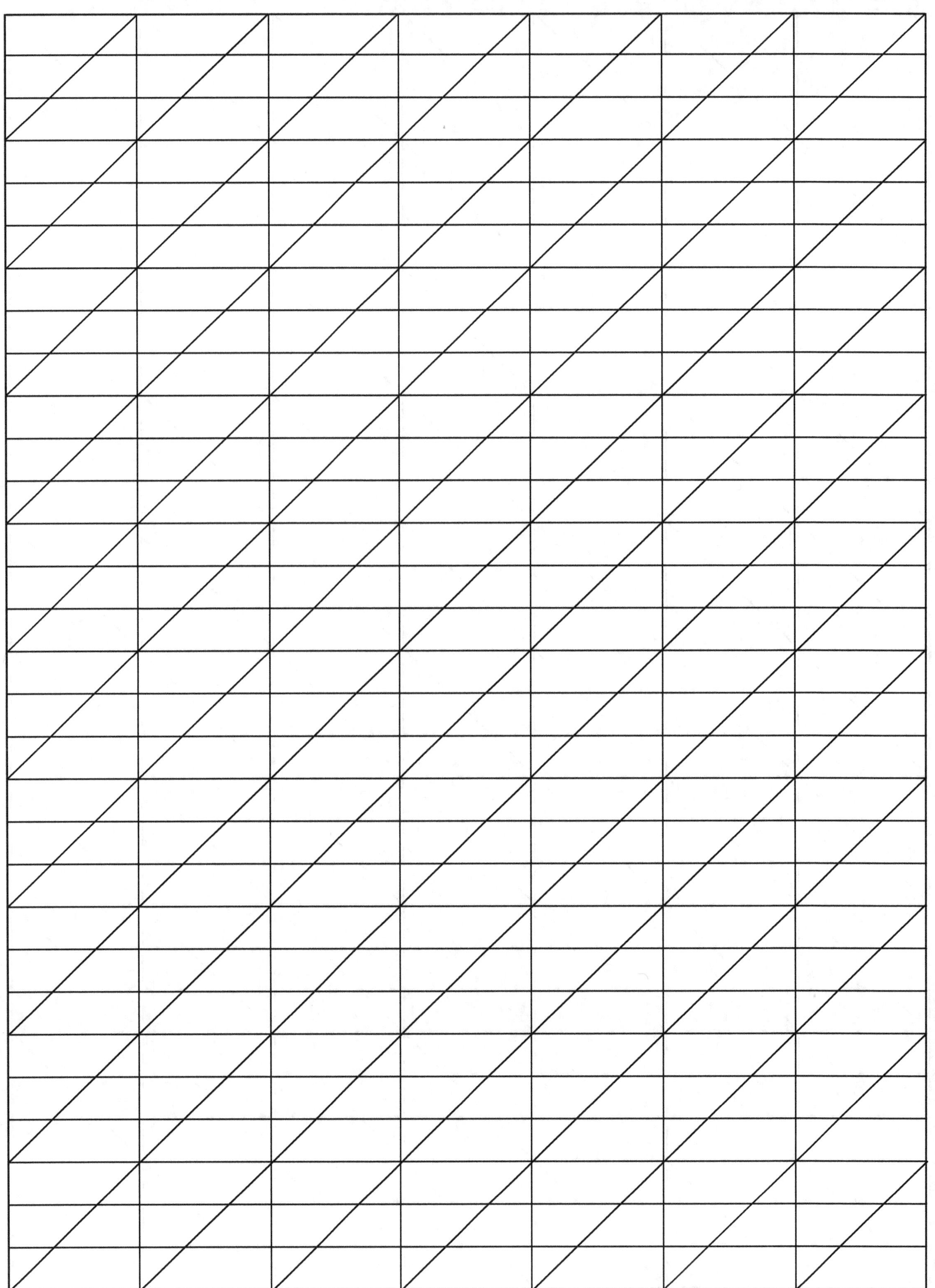

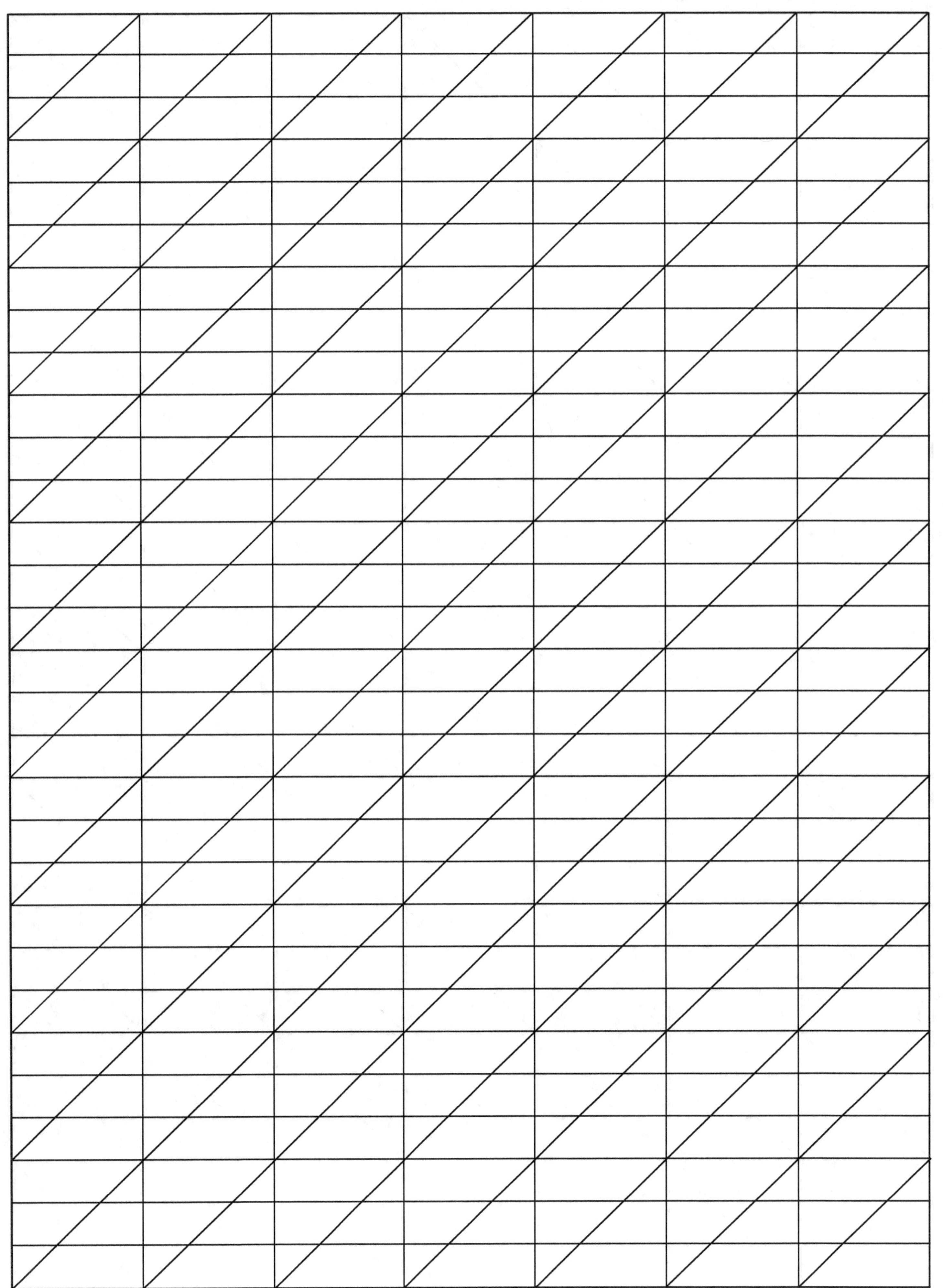

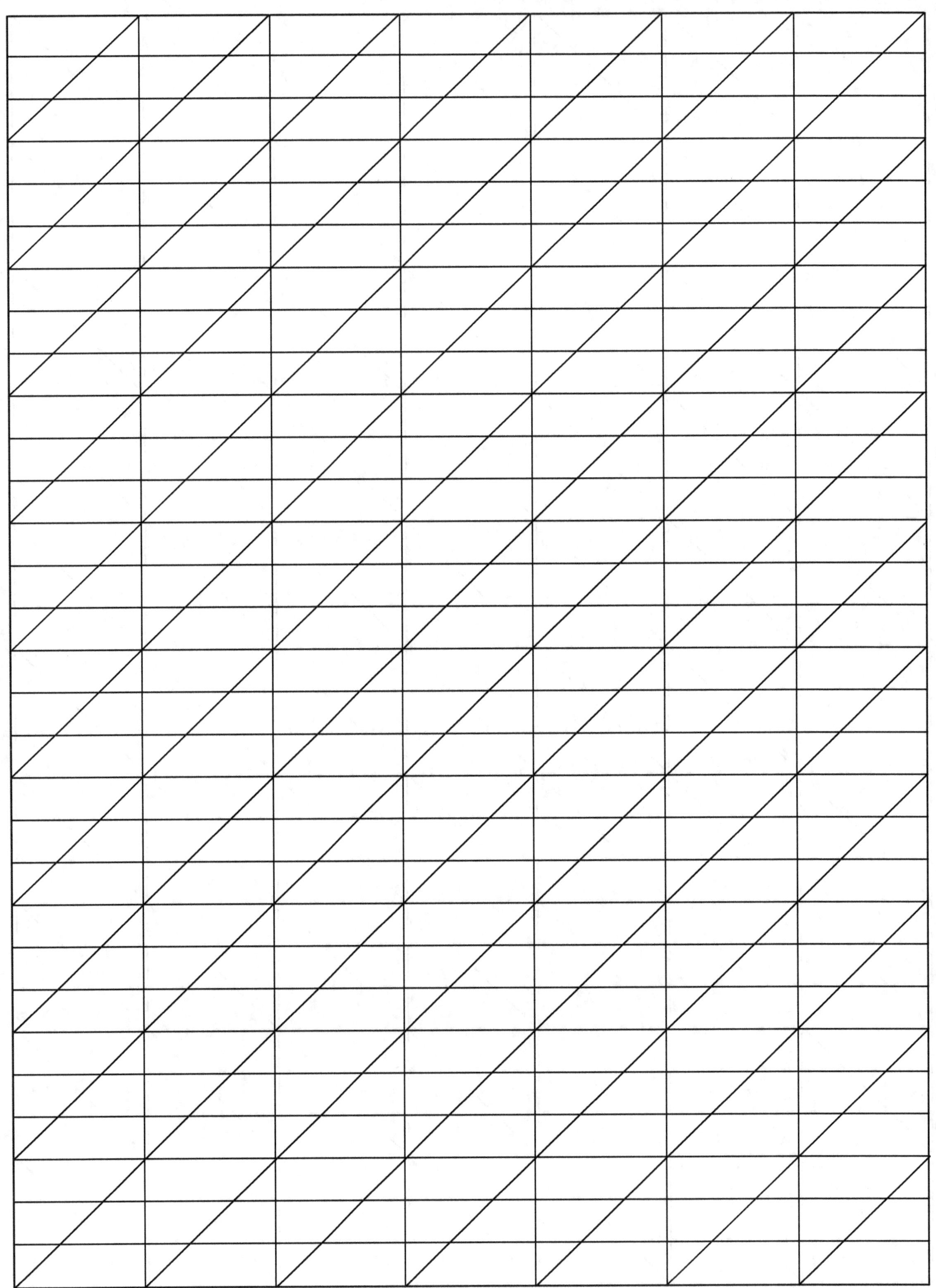

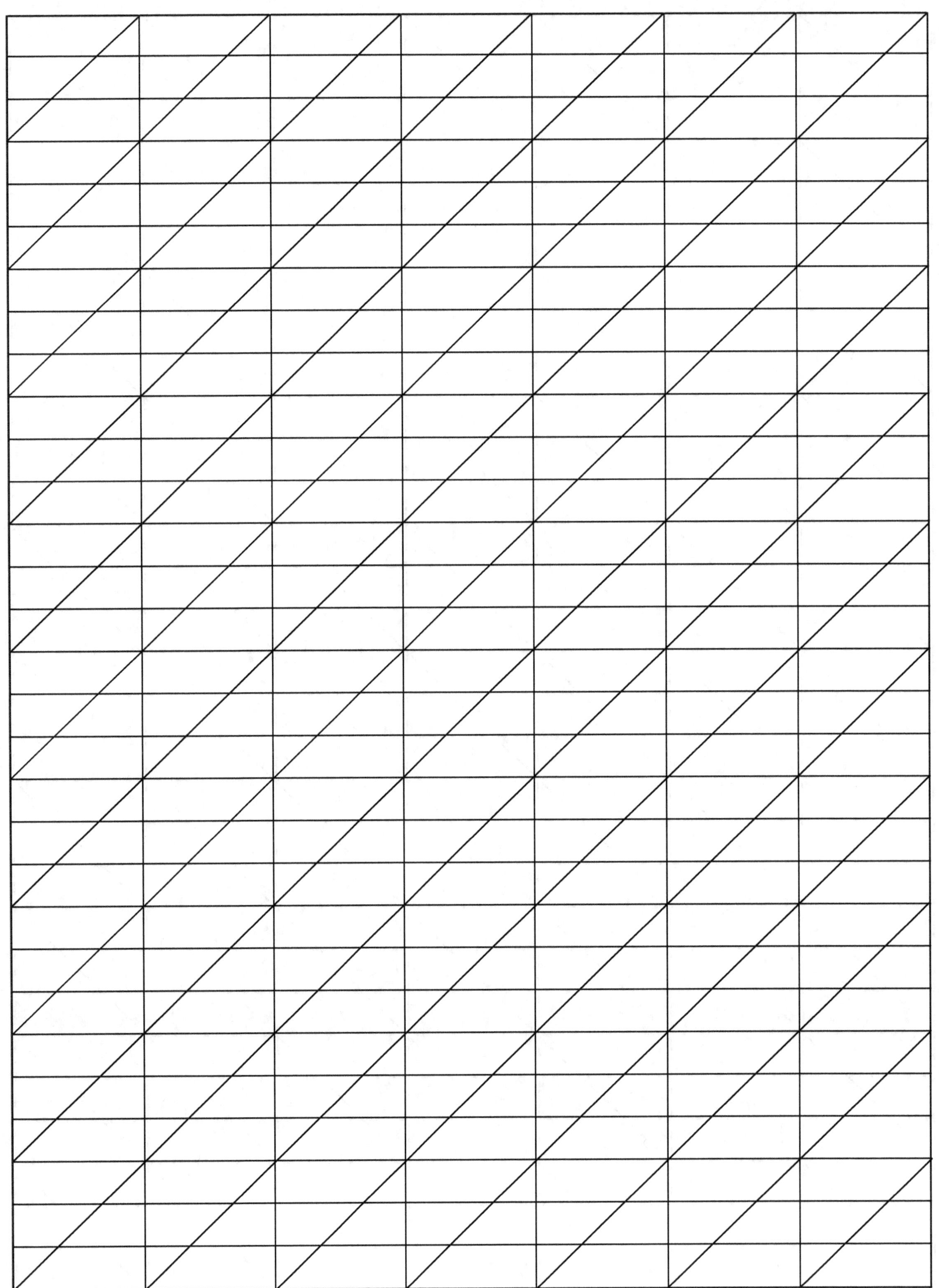

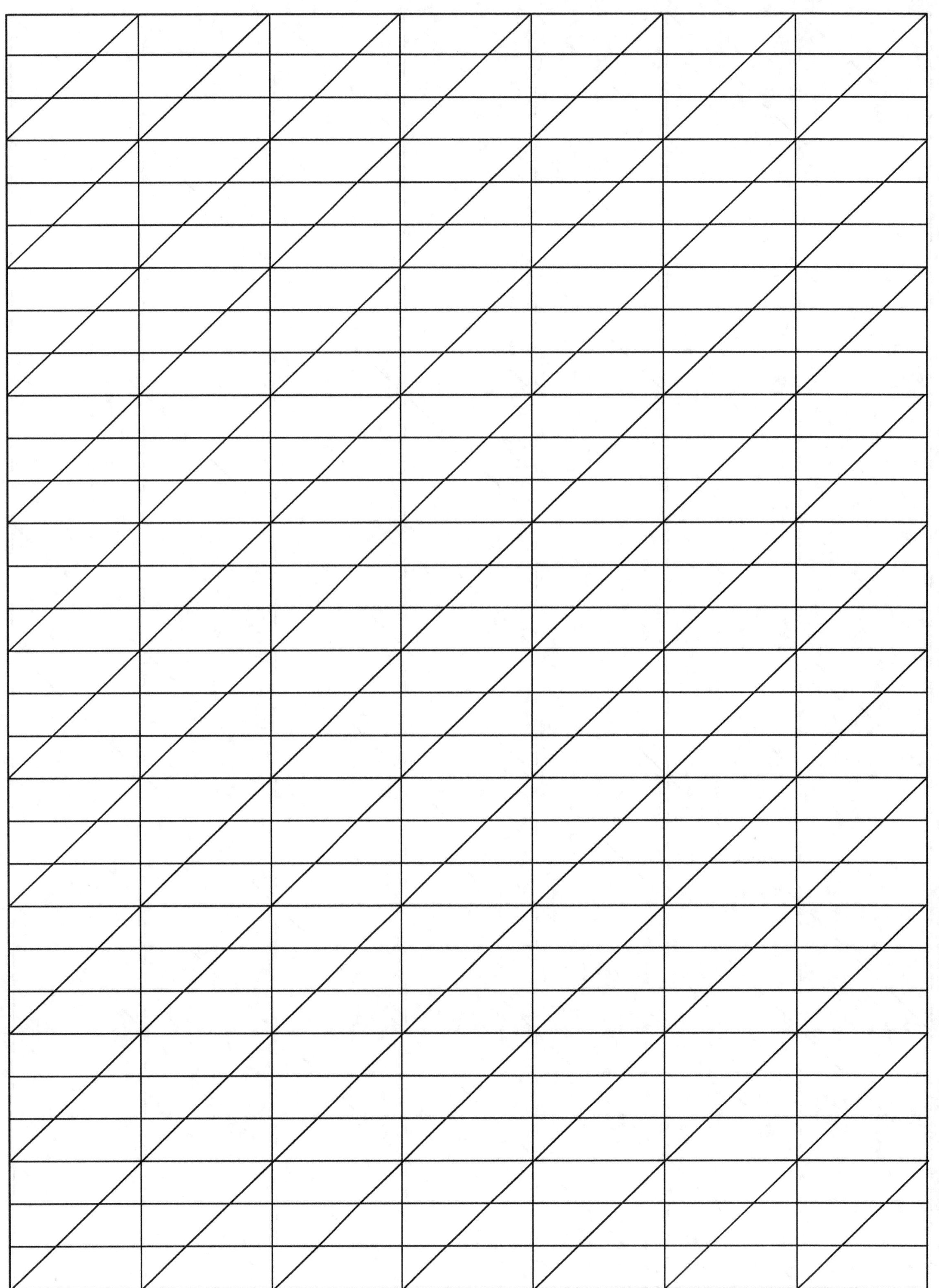

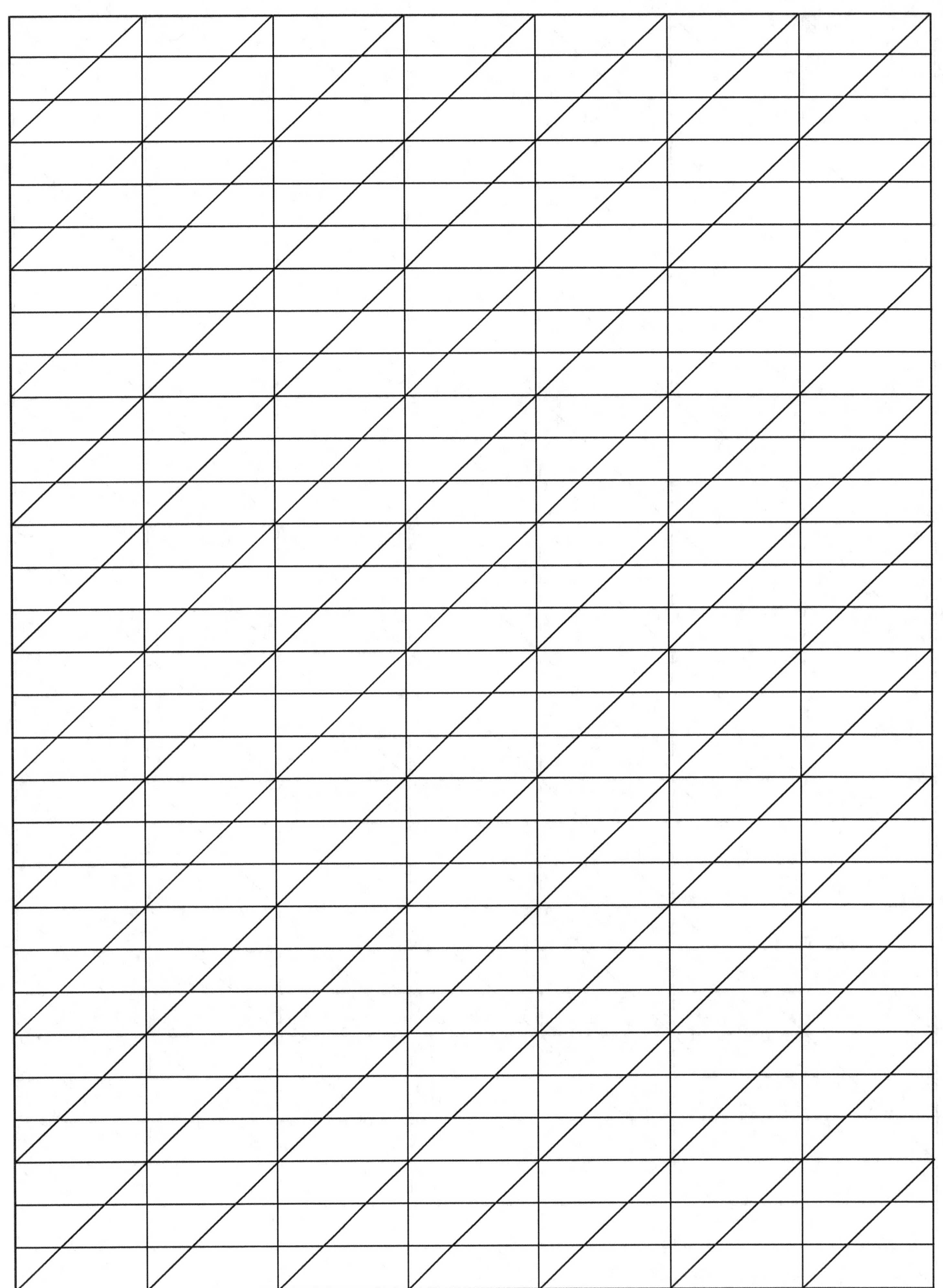

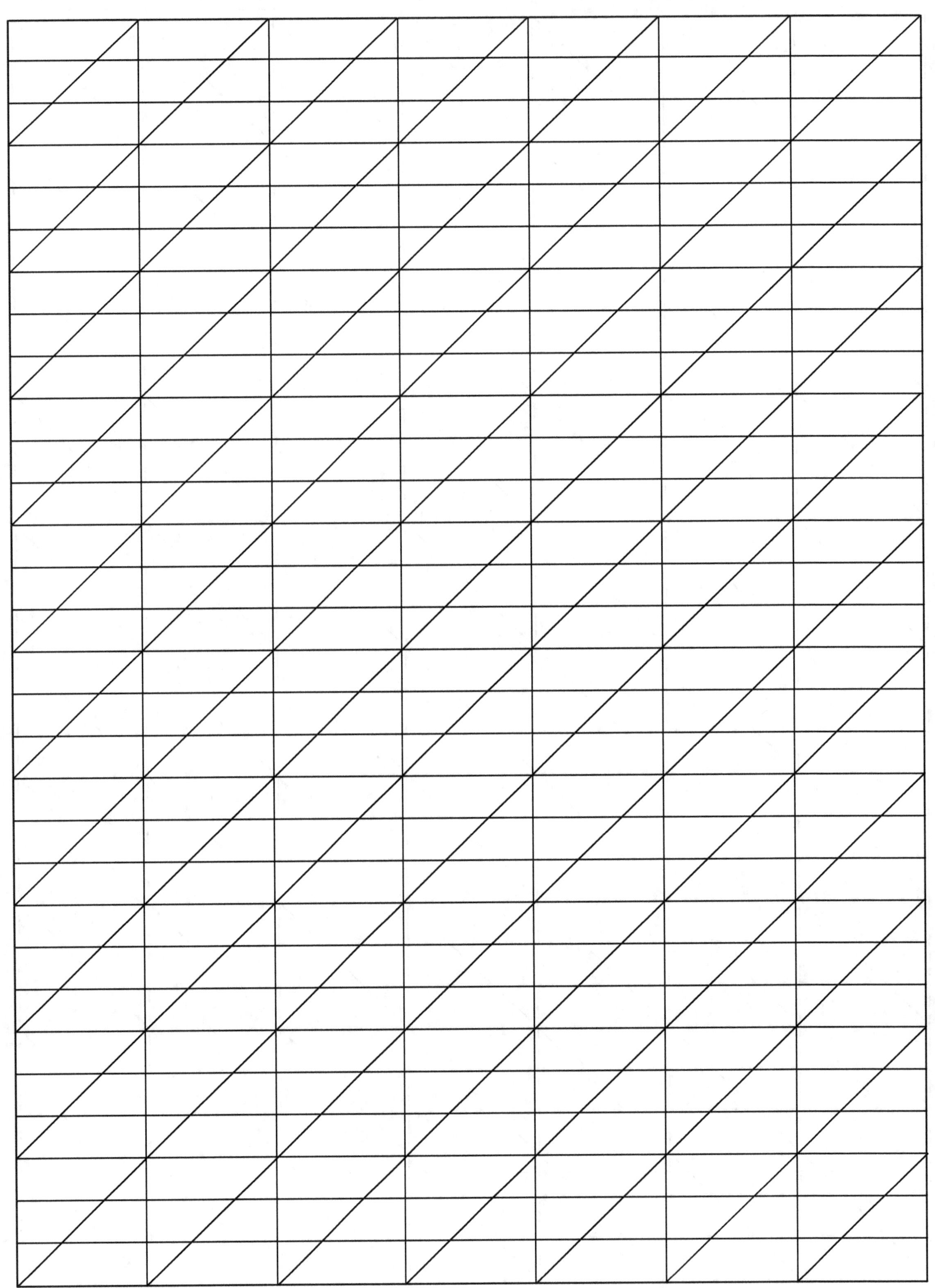

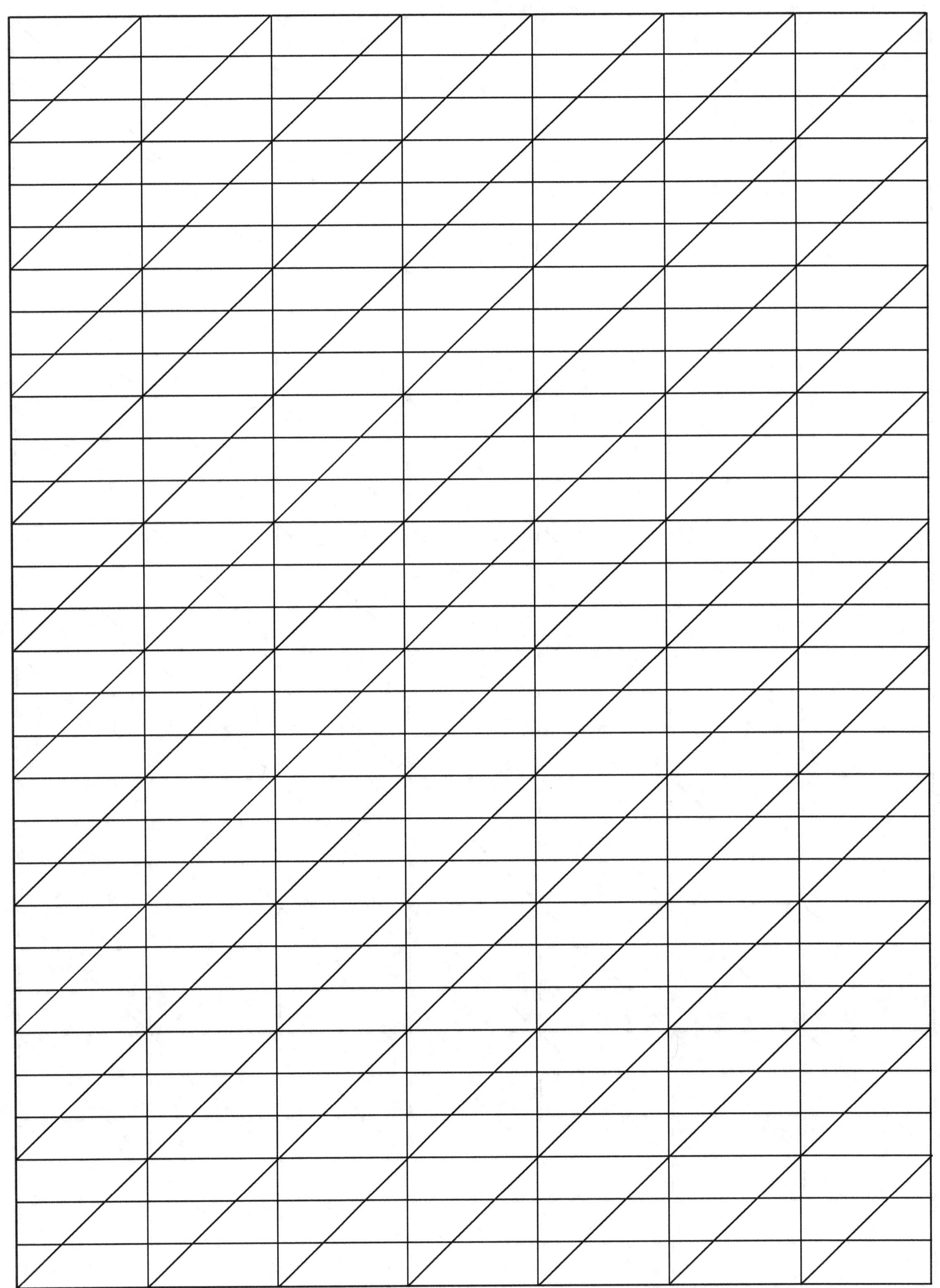

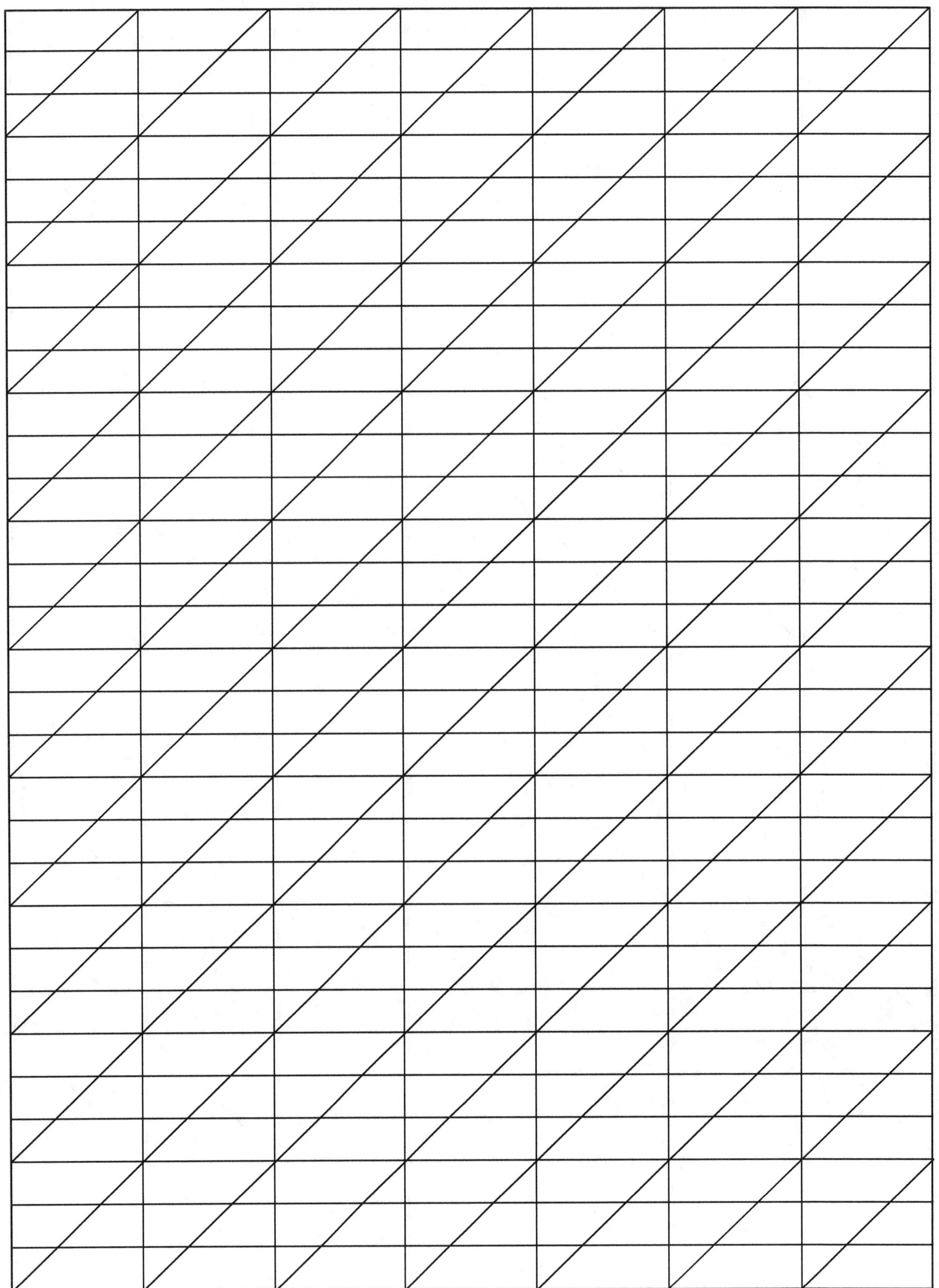

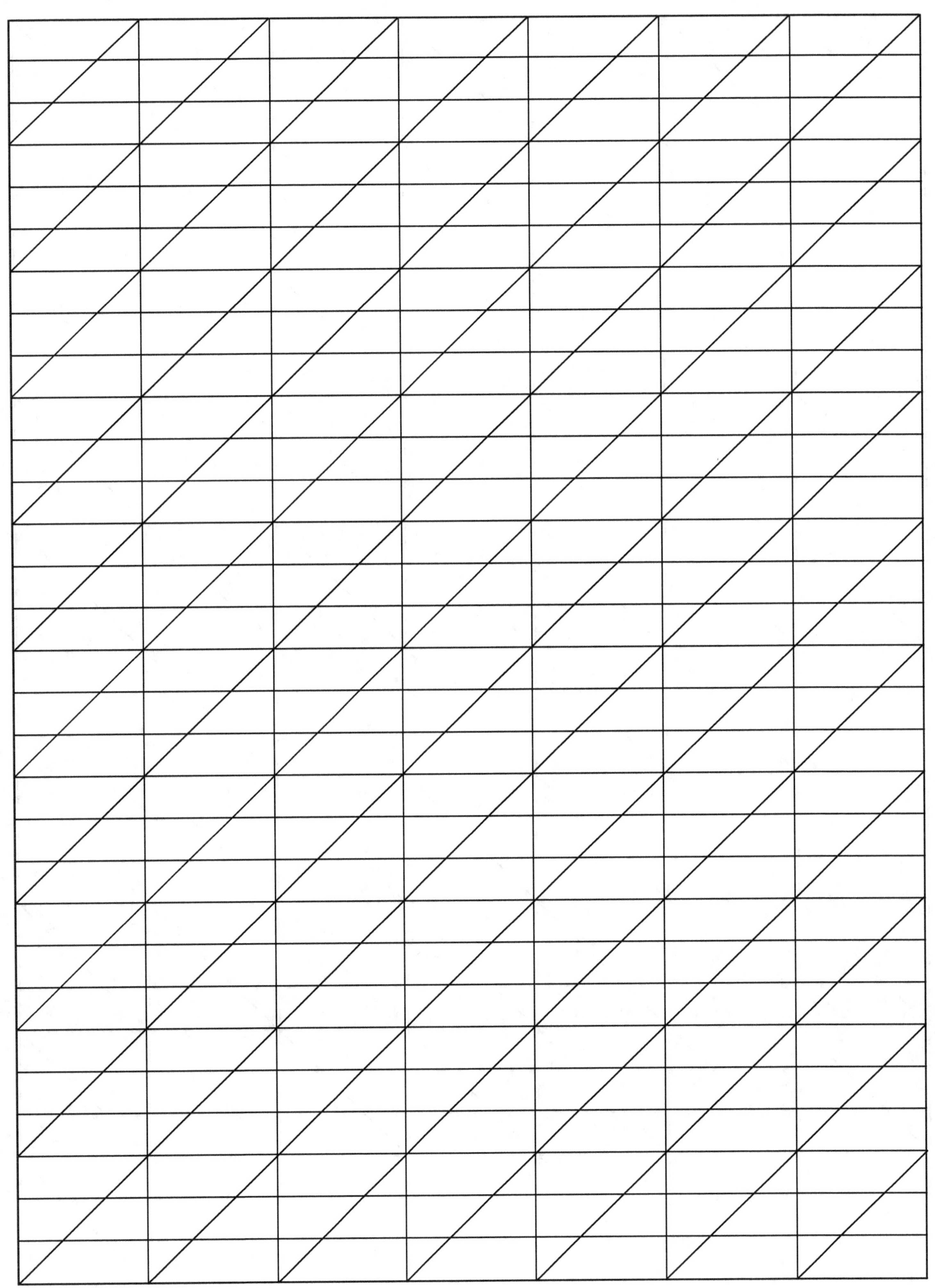

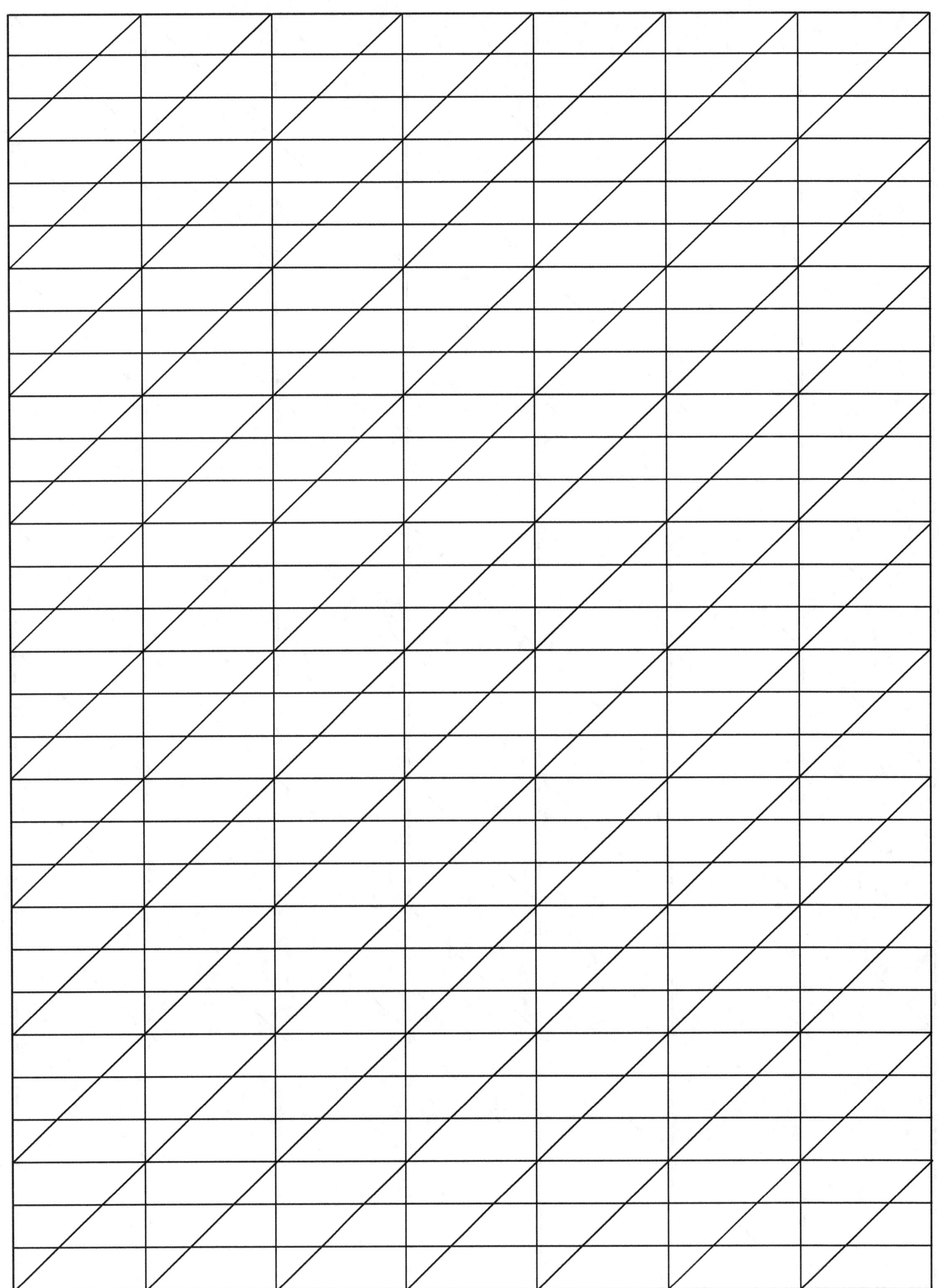

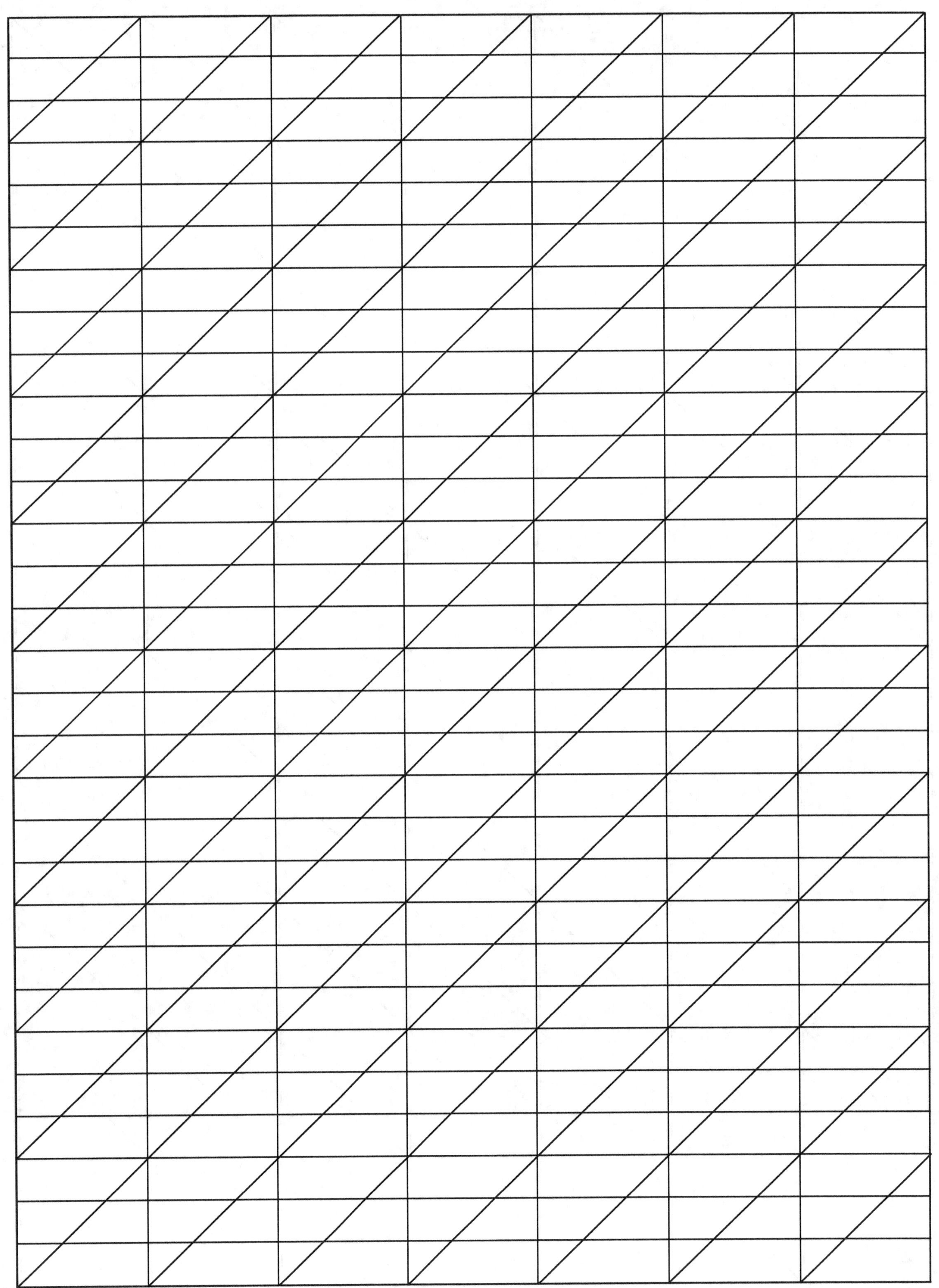

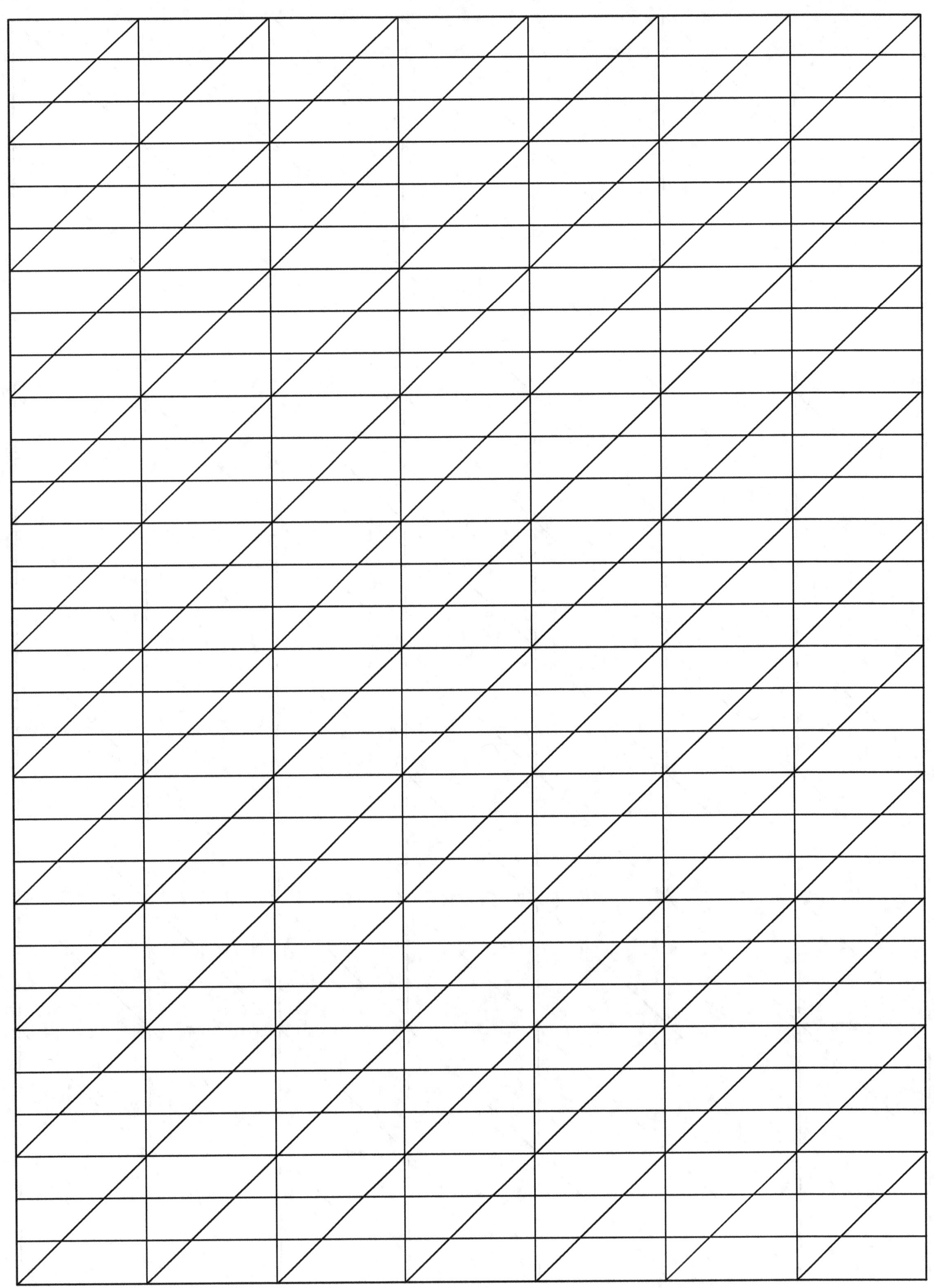

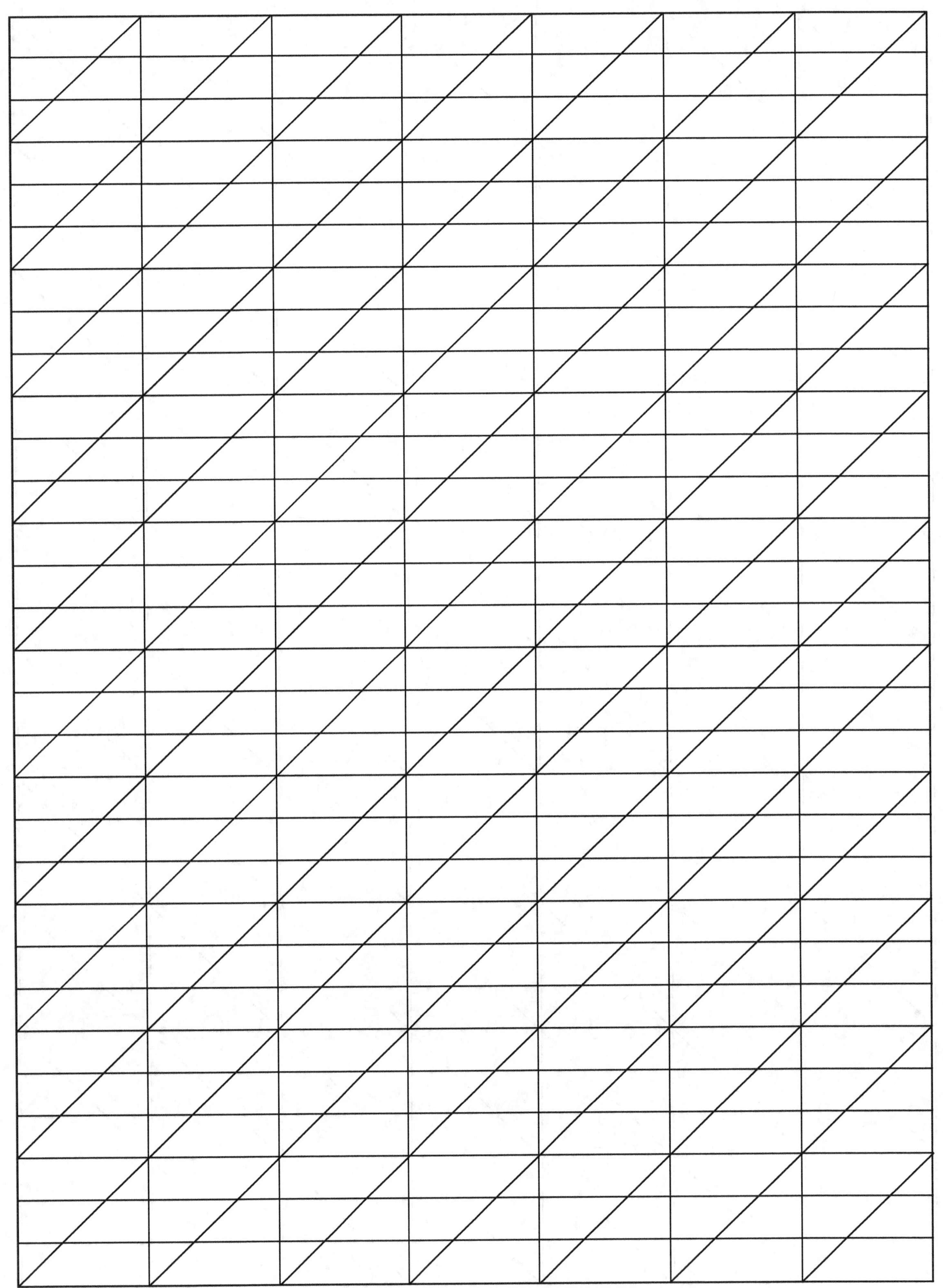

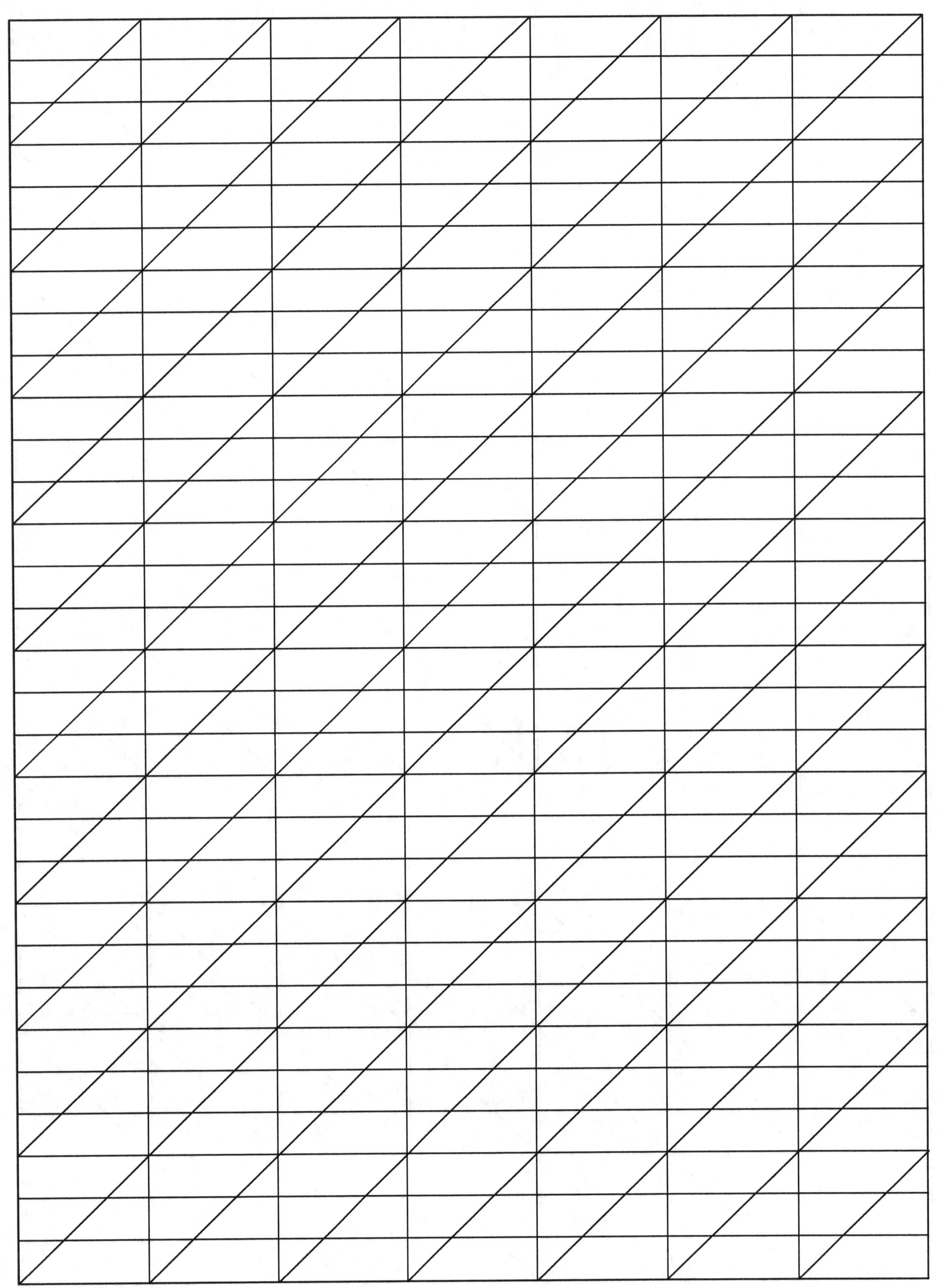

I want to thank
You for
purchasing This
Book. I would be
very grateful for
taking a moment
and leaving
feedback. It
helps our small
business grow and
reach more
people.